D0354157

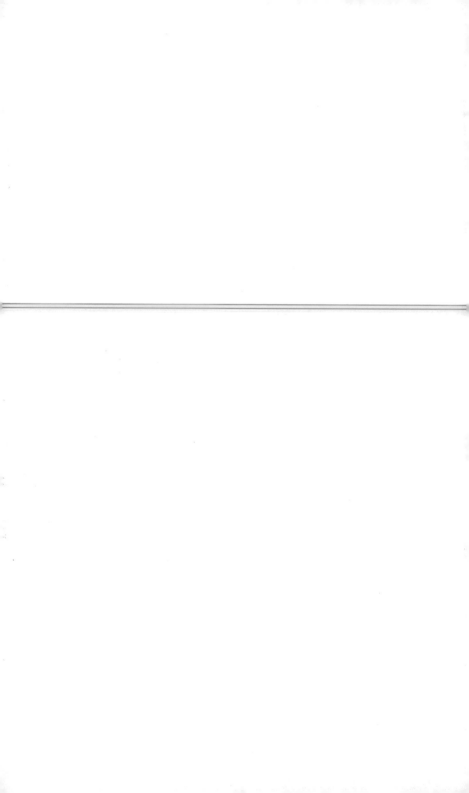

ADVANCE PRAISE FOR *ONE AND ONLY*

"*One and Only* is essential reading for anyone wishing to get the full picture of the Beat Generation. Lu Anne Henderson was Neal Cassady's lifelong love and was responsible for the friendship with Kerouac that gave us *On the Road*. Gerald Nicosia was always a loyal advocate of the women of the Beat Generation, and his remarkable interview with Lu Anne fills in an enormous gap in the story. It shows the vulnerability and insecurities of the main characters, and reveals the chaos of their emotional lives so that Kerouac and company finally emerge as real people! A great book."

—Barry Miles, author of *Jack Kerouac: King of the Beats*

"Gerald Nicosia is Kerouac's best biographer. Critics unanimously praised *Memory Babe* for its honesty, its broad, deep research, its narrative style, and its respect for and understanding of Jack Kerouac. Now he gives us a different kind of book in *One and Only*. I am fascinated by characters in fiction who live outside of the book and confront us in real life. Nicosia found Lu Anne Henderson and listened to her voice with great care. He's written the context, made room so that she can tell *her* truth about *On the Road*. We go again but differently on that mythic road with Jack and Neal."

—Maxine Hong Kingston, author of *The Woman Warrior*

"*One and Only* is an ongoing chapter in the riveting Beat saga, chronicling another life and its poignant hopes and fears. An unsung teen-heroine of the time, Lu Anne Henderson, the young woman on whom the character 'Marylou' in *On the Road* is based, finally has her say. The book is an intimate and revealing portrait in the annals of American belletristic and real-life memory."

—Anne Waldman, author of *Beats at Naropa* and co-founder of
The Jack Kerouac School of Disembodied Poetics, Naropa University

"Gerald Nicosia performs a fascinating feat of balance with *One and Only*. While preserving his admiration for Jack Kerouac's writing, he explores—with the collaboration of Anne Marie Santos and the preserved words of Lu Anne Henderson—the faults of character which contribute to an ambiguous cult status for Jack Kerouac and his beau ideal, Neal Cassady. The book is a most valuable addition to Kerouaciana and the legend of Neal Cassady. It also gives Lu Anne a place she deserves, and has not gotten from others."

—Herbert Gold, author of *Bohemia*

"It takes a Zen-like skill to tightrope-walk the 60 years of complexity and rumor that lay across Beat legends Jack Kerouac and Neal Cassady. Gerald Nicosia effortlessly performs the feat using his interviews with Cassady's first wife, Lu Anne, as his point of entry. Nicosia has a historian's vision that generously accommodates the ambivalences and Rashomon quality of memory. With a breezy and genuine beatitude, Nicosia renders the pre-*On the Road* Beat world with an admiration that doesn't discount its occasional irony and fraud. *One and Only* is a book of masterful craft subversively camouflaged as coolly minimal in which the sophisticated tricks of the trade of fiction are used to tell a real story."

—Kate Braverman, author of
Lithium for Medea, *Palm Latitudes*, and *Squandering the Blue*

"This is the missing back-story of the back-story of *On the Road*, the mysterious missing woman a lot of us sensed was there but invisible and silent. Until now. Nicosia has given her voice and made her visible, and she's extraordinary. No wonder both Kerouac and Cassady loved her."

—Russell Banks, author of *Cloudsplitter*

"Gerald Nicosia has done it again! He just keeps filling in the pieces of the Beat era for us. *One and Only* fleshes out the beginnings of *On the Road* and makes it fuller and more interesting. Lu Anne was certainly a force to be reckoned with. Her lust for life and fullness of being and generosity of spirit show through only too clearly. Her vital North Beach career, her mothering ability, her recovery from heroin addiction, her many marriages, her long clandestine affair with Neal, and her own longevity speak well for her love affair with life as well as with Neal. And her demand for a 'broad margin to her life,' showing she had 'as much right to go through every open door as a man had,' will strike many women as apt in their own lives. By the 60s, a number of us followed her. I read *One and Only* from cover to cover in one day, and Lu Anne's presence hovers with me still."

—Joanna McClure, original Beat poet, author of *Extended Love Poem*

"I read *One and Only* straight through and loved it, and loved the energy that was put into it. Lu Anne, much ignored by most of the biographers except Nicosia, finally comes across as a vital part of the Beat Generation. His new book is an informative and moving portrait of a girl who was really a lady, and lets us see once again how strong was the influence of womanhood on the major Beats, both negative and positive. *One and Only* is must reading and fills in many gaps. It will become an essential part of the Beat canon."

—Jerry Kamstra, original Beat poet, author of *The Frisco Kid*

"Gerry Nicosia is to the Beat Generation what Alan Lomax was to the history of the blues, the voice-catcher of his generation. In *One and Only*, written in collaboration with Anne Marie Santos, Nicosia reveals the story behind the story of the great American epic, *On the Road*, which is to say he uncovers one of its deeply buried secrets. Every myth has one, and the great unknown force that brought Jack Kerouac and Neal Cassady together is revealed here for the first time in the vivacious voice of the vixen Lu Anne Henderson. Reading her story is like riding with her in the backseat on one of those long, bluesy romps across the great heartland. *Go, go, go...*"

— Phil Cousineau, author of *Wordcatcher* and *The Book of Roads*

"The voice of Lu Anne Henderson rises up off the page in this tender yet psychologically acute memoir, transcribed by Gerald Nicosia from tapes he made thirty years ago. Henderson played a crucial, inspirational part in the lives of Cassady and Kerouac, and the true circumstances of their complex relationship are revealed here for the first time. *One and Only* also shows the poverty and chaos and sometimes the sheer scariness of the lives of the Beats. Above all, the book shows the vulnerability and lack of self-esteem, the confusion and jealousy, which lay behind Cassady and Kerouac's machismo. Henderson's crucial insight is that Cassady and Kerouac, despite their profound friendship, were 'totally unaware of the other one's real feelings,' a situation which only got worse when they became cultural icons. This new book by Nicosia is an invaluable contribution to Beat history."

—Ian MacFadyen, editor of *Naked Lunch at 50: Anniversary Essays*

"What a great and important find: Lu Anne Henderson, aka Marylou of *On the Road*. Neglected by most of the scholarship, she put Jack and Neal together, is at the core of the movement that changed history, both literary and cultural history. But only Eastern establishment scholars and male-identified fans could be stunned by her. For Westerners, childhood was full of such women—the mothers we grew from. Henderson's authenticity is no surprise—is relief, joy, and truth. We owe thanks to Gerald Nicosia for the interestingly-crafted *One and Only*, a sweet book and a delightful, beautiful story that can never again be ignored."

—Sharon Doubiago, author of *Love on the Streets*

"In *One and Only*, Gerald Nicosia is a man burning with a story to tell like no other told before: the true story of the pre-legendary men and women upon whom the classic postwar novel *On the Road*'s characters were modeled. Nicosia's sturdily edited portrait of Lu Anne Henderson from lengthy taped interviews and his dramatic and accurate narration of Lu Anne's life amongst the *ur*-Beats and thereafter, with the help of her daughter Anne Santos, bring to light as never before the human dimensions of those lives before they were iconic. Lu Anne's life was not about Neal Cassady or Kerouac or any of them; her story is her humanity. Now, with Gerald Nicosia's *One and Only*, a master of living Beat history has brought to life for the first time a 'Beat woman' who was a woman, first of all."

—James Grauerholz, editor of
Word Virus: The William S. Burroughs Reader

"Just as the Beats were the missing link between the bohemians and the hippies, so was lovely Lu Anne the missing link between Cassady and Kerouac. In this book, she reveals how they played the roles that were expected of them, and then expected by themselves, until finally their roles began to play them. Gerald Nicosia provides a backstage pass to a unique era of foibles and follies that range from poignant to preposterous, so that *One and Only* does indeed live up to its name."

—Paul Krassner, author of *Confessions of a Raving,*
Unconfined Nut: Misadventures in the Counterculture

"I always sensed Lu Anne was Neal's real sweetheart. He always had a special look on his face when he mouthed her name. Having been an intimate of major players in that generation, I am drawn to anecdotal, primary narratives like *One and Only*. For me, they're more interesting than the fictions like *On the Road*. *One and Only* reveals a good deal about the gene pool in that fabulous era. In Lu Anne's life, as in the larger culture, cool changed from hep to hip. This book reveals the spark, in flesh, of another holder of the flame."

—Charles Plymell, author of
The Last of the Moccasins and friend of Neal Cassady

"*One and Only* is an essential addition and corrective to the masculine locus of Beat Generation history. Lu Anne Henderson was a witness and participant in the legendary road trips and saw Neal Cassady, Kerouac, Ginsberg, and Burroughs in a clear-headed light. Nicosia's reclamation of her centrality to that experience is revelatory. Her testimony captures her complicated involvement with these men with clarity, compassion, and wise humor. This book is a necessary revelation of the female experience in postwar United States, not to mention the incredible story and insights into the times covered by *On the Road* and also the period afterward."

—David Meltzer, original Beat poet, author of
San Francisco Beats: Talking with the Poets

"There have always been great women behind the important men of our collective literary existence. Lu Anne Henderson (Cassady) was the apocalyptic spark behind the rowdy duo of Jack Kerouac and Neal Cassady. According to the new book *One and Only* by Gerald Nicosia, a vital addition to the historical archives of Beat consciousness, Neal and Jack didn't get along with each other before Lu Anne connected them. Nicosia, one of our most important Beat chroniclers, here delves into places other researchers have left untouched. *One and Only* exposes the liveliness and magnetic charms of a beautiful woman with a beautiful soul, who led a fascinating yet problematic life."

—Tony Rodriguez, author of *When I Followed the Elephant*

"In *One and Only*, Gerald Nicosia treats Jack Kerouac with the respect he has always shown for this great writer, just as he has always been a friend and supporter of the real Kerouac family. It's an extremely well-done book, in which we see the *On the Road* story through other people's eyes, in a way that is sometimes painful and sometimes humorous, but always definitely real. In Jack Kerouac's own spirit, Nicosia gives us the full, no-holds-barred telling of a story we only heard parts of before."

—Paul Blake, Jr., Jack Kerouac's nephew

ONE AND ONLY

ONE AND ONLY

THE UNTOLD STORY OF
ON THE ROAD

AND LU ANNE HENDERSON,
THE WOMAN WHO STARTED JACK KEROUAC
AND NEAL CASSADY ON THEIR JOURNEY

GERALD NICOSIA

AND

ANNE MARIE SANTOS

Viva
EDITIONS

Published in the United States by Viva Editions,
an imprint of Cleis Press, Inc., 2246 Sixth Street, Berkeley, California 94710.

Printed in the United States.
Cover design: Scott Idleman
Front cover photo of Jack Kerouac and Neal Cassady by Al Hinkle.
Front cover photo of Lu Anne Henderson courtesy of Anne Marie Santos.
Text design: Frank Wiedemann
First Edition.
10 9 8 7 6 5 4 3 2 1

Hardcover ISBN: 978-1-936740-04-8
E-book ISBN: 978-1-936740-09-3

Photo on p. 12 courtesy of Anne Marie Santos.

Library of Congress Cataloging-in-Publication Data

Nicosia, Gerald.
 One and only : the untold story of On the road and Lu Anne Henderson, the woman who started Jack Kerouac and Neal Cassady on their journey / by Gerald Nicosia and Anne Marie Santos. -- 1st ed.
    p. cm.
 ISBN 978-1-936740-04-8 (hardcover)
 1. Kerouac, Jack, 1922-1969--Friends and associates. 2. Henderson, Lu Anne. 3. Cassady, Neal. 4. Cassady, Carolyn. 5. Kerouac, Jack, 1922-1969. On the road 6. Beat generation. 7. Heroin abuse. I. Santos, Anne Marie. II. Title.
 PS3521.E735Z794 2011
 813'.54--dc23
 [B]
                                    2011031407

To my very own Doris Day
Mother, I love you. "Que sera, sera."
—A.M.S.

To Sylvia Anna Fremer Nicosia,
known as "San,"
and all the mothers who try to make
a better world for their children
—G.N.

We'll be together, you are my one and only wife.
—Neal Cassady to Lu Anne Cassady

Acknowledgments

⸺➤◦◄⸺

O f course, my first thanks go out to the spirit of Lu Anne Henderson Cassady. If she hadn't granted me those two interviews, neither this book nor a whole lot else would exist. Thanks of course to Larry Lee, too, another angel who got his wings the hard way. It was Larry's act of kindness in sharing Lu Anne's whereabouts with me that opened the door for me with her in the first place. A big thanks to Walter Salles and the entire cast and crew of the movie *On the Road*. If Walter hadn't asked me to be part of the initial work on that film, I would not have listened again to that full seven-and-a-half-hour taped interview, which had been locked up in an archive in Lowell, Massachusetts, for many years, beyond everyone's reach. My work as an advisor to Walter and other crew members, especially Kristen Stewart, Sam Riley, and Garrett Hedlund, helped me focus my own thoughts about Lu Anne.

There is no way I can adequately express my enormous debt to Lu Anne's daughter, Anne Marie Santos, who allowed me to put my brief experience with Lu Anne in a far larger and longer context. By the same token, I have to thank Al Hinkle and his daughter Dawn Hinkle Davis for their great generosity in sharing stories that added vastly to the richness of the narrative. My editor and publisher, Brenda Knight, was a *sine qua non* of this project, as were the core staff members of Cleis Press and its co-publishers Felice Newman and Frédérique Delacoste. Thanks to so many others who contributed photographs and other key pieces of the puzzle—including, especially, photographers Jerry Bauer, James Oliver Mitchell, and Larry Keenan, Jr., who by themselves and on little funding documented a wide swath of America's germinating counterculture. Thanks to my family, of course—Ellen, Amy, and Peter—for support and patience during my work on the book. And thanks most of all to the angelic spirits of Jack Kerouac and Neal Cassady—not for getting us all into this mess, but for showing us the beginning of a way out. *Pax vobiscum* to that whole ragtag bunch called the Beat Generation.

—G.N.

* * *

First thank-you goes to Gerry Nicosia for reaching out to me and guiding me through this amazing experience.

To Brenda Knight and all those at Cleis Press and Viva Editions who believed in this project.

Thank you to my love Reuben (TT&F), to Katie, Erin, Mason, and Mia, without whom I could not exist.

To all the women in my family who came before, onward we go.

Most importantly, to Mother and my daughter Melissa, the bravest and most loving of women, and I was the lucky one loved by both. Thank you.

—*Annie Ree*

Contents

INTRODUCTION

THE NECESSARY ESTROGEN

———————⟶•◦•⟵———————

B ack in 1978, when I was traveling around the country doing interviews for my biography *Memory Babe*, there was a lot going on in the Kerouac realm. New Kerouac biographies were in the works by both Dennis McNally and the team of Barry Gifford and Larry Lee, but the hottest action was going on down in Hollywood—the filming of Carolyn Cassady's memoir *Heart Beat* with such stars as Nick Nolte, Sissy Spacek, and John Heard. I counted myself lucky to be a friend of Carolyn's, and through her I wangled an invitation to the set down in Culver City in early October of that year. I had just missed seeing my new friend Jan Kerouac, Jack's daughter, there. I'd also managed to connect her and Carolyn, so that Jan got a bit part in the film—a part that was, unbelievably, left on the cutting-room floor. Jan was working on a memoir too, as were Jack's ex-wives Edie Parker and Joan Haverty, as well as his quondam girlfriends Joyce Johnson and Helen Weaver. The women were surfacing, though it would be almost two more decades before they got their due in Brenda Knight's landmark book, *Women of the Beat Generation*, as well as Richard Peabody's lesser-known but equally important *A Different Beat*. One woman had notably been absent from all this neo-Beat hullabaloo, the woman every Kerouac fan knew as "Marylou" from *On the Road*: Lu Anne Henderson Cassady. No one had heard from her in a long time. No one seemed to know where to find her.

Then one day, while I was still out in California, I got a call from Larry Lee. Larry deserves remembering here. A Peabody-award-winning journalist for KRON television in the Bay Area, he was one of the first prominent gay men in San Francisco to die from that epidemic that would take so many thousands of lives out here—including, a little later, the tremendous writer Randy Shilts. It troubles me to see how quickly Larry Lee's name has been forgotten in the Bay Area, and how people now routinely ask "Who?" when his name is mentioned. Time buries us all, but maybe those who die young get buried quicker, having had less time to leave a testament to their memory.

Larry was short, slender, with a walrus mustache and a pixieish smile. But his brown eyes could burn into you when he was after some critical information. He had one of the sharpest minds I had yet encountered, and he was nobody's fool. But one thing stands out about him in my memory more than any other. Of all the Kerouac critics, scholars, and biographers running around then—and running in ever larger numbers nowadays, in veritable wolf packs, in fact—he was the only totally noncompetitive one I knew. Maybe he could afford to be noncompetitive because he was a journalist, only on the periphery of those bloody fields of literary combat, where every writer seems out to climb a step higher on the backs of his brothers. But I don't really think that was it. Larry was just a kind man—that was the essential thing about him. When I first came out to the Bay Area and had no money to live on, he cashed a check for me that no one else would touch. When you looked at his face, you saw some past hurt there that had left him with a deep compassion for the whole human race, but I never knew him well enough to find out what that hurt had been.

Larry called me around the middle of October, just as I was getting set to return to my mother's house in a Chicago suburb named Lyons, which was my home base at that time, the place where I was finally beginning to turn years of research into the thousands of lines of inked typeface that would eventually become *Memory Babe*. "I know where Lu Anne is," Larry told me. "Would you like to know?" Was the pope Catholic?

Lu Anne, as it turned out, was at that very moment in San Francisco General Hospital. As much as I wanted to interview her, she was in no condition to endure a barrage of questions while I ran a tape recorder on her; but she could receive visitors, I was told. Larry may have spoken to her about me—I don't remember. I had also recently interviewed her good friend Al Hinkle. That might have helped too. I don't remember all the steps exactly, but she consented to see me, and I got down to San Francisco General as fast as my rental car would carry me.

San Francisco General, for those who don't know, is not a hospital for the rich and privileged. It is a place where insuranceless patients routinely get shuffled, where bloodied gang members routinely get treated. It also, later, became a center of treatment and mercy for the hordes of needy sick during the AIDS epidemic. It is a large gray building with numerous wings down at the base of Potrero Hill, in the less-than-fashionable southern annex of San Francisco. The staff there are notoriously dedicated, and the atmosphere in the hospital has always been one of cordiality and heartfelt helpfulness.

I entered Lu Anne's hospital room not knowing what I would find. Those years of cross-country travel and hundreds of interviews had been a dizzying roller coaster, meeting crazy alcoholic barroom bruisers who threatened my life, and a few poets who threatened my life too, as well as some of the loveliest, sweetest people in the world, people who were ready to do anything to help someone (me) write the truth about their late friend or relative Jack Kerouac. What I saw was a large (larger than I'd expected), beautiful fortyish woman with a full head of blonde curls, in a blue hospital gown, with one hand swathed completely in white bandages, giving me the softest, kindest, most understanding smile I'd seen in a long, long time. She was absolutely radiant, beaming at me with an expression of gentleness and intelligence that reminded me of various Marys I had seen in the Catholic churches of my boyhood. I think I was a little in love with her before she even spoke.

I told her who I was, that I wanted to talk to her about Jack Kerouac for the book I was writing. Then a look of sadness crossed her face, and she told me that too many people wanted to learn about her life, and the lives of her friends, but it didn't seem like anybody really wanted to know why she and her friends had done the things they did. To her, the most important thing was finding out why people acted in certain ways. Once you understood them, she felt, their actions almost always made perfect sense. They stopped being freaks or criminals or outcasts or whatever else the world had labeled them as, and they became instead someone like yourself—a friend. It baffled her, it truly did, that so many writers, as well as the legions of Beat trekkies that were beginning to hit the roads of America, were smitten by the flashy and often trashy surface of the Beat movement, but had failed to understand—actually seemed incapable of understanding—that the Beats were ordinary people, just as they were.

Lu Anne told me that she had recently visited the set of Carolyn's movie *Heart Beat*, and that she was enormously disappointed by what she had seen there. The first thing she saw—in a scene being filmed—was Ann Dusenberry, the actress who was playing her, supposedly peeing in a washbowl and then calling for a towel. "I wasn't a slob," Lu Anne objected, "and besides, there's no need to show something like that. There's no redeeming value in that."

Then she watched the filming of a scene where Sissy Spacek, playing Carolyn Cassady, comes into a hotel room in Denver and acts "so indignant" to find Neal (Nolte), Lu Anne, and Allen Ginsberg (Ray Sharkey) all in bed together. "What did *she* have to be indignant about?" Lu Anne asked me. "After all, Neal was *my* husband—not hers, *yet*." Lu Anne winked at me, and a wry smile crossed her face. I was beginning to get the sense that she was a bit of a card, as they used to say. For the past few months, I had been spending quite a bit of time with Carolyn Cassady. I liked Carolyn, but she could be a bit pompous and ponderous with her lectures on Edgar Cayce, karmic debts, and reincarnation. Carolyn did not have much of a sense of humor, and not at all the sort of quick humor that Lu Anne had.

Lu Anne told me more about the reenactment of that infamous three-way sex scene in *Heart Beat*. She felt the director, John Byrum, had done his best to make it seem as tawdry and kinky as possible. "When the three of us went to bed together," Lu Anne said, "Neal always used to be in the middle, and Allen and I would be on either side of him. The two or three times we all actually had sex together, it was very nice." She smiled again at me—not the wry smile, but almost the Mother Mary smile again. "There was nothing obscene about the sex we had with each other—nothing you couldn't show on a screen or that you'd need more than a PG-13 rating for," she averred.

Of course she won me over that quickly. I had never known any women like Lu Anne, who could talk so easily about sex and yet also make it seem so natural and healthy, nothing to be ashamed of or to make a big deal about at all. She was as at ease talking about sex as she was talking about anything else in her life. Remember, this was a good two decades before we had a program like *Sex and the City*. And always, everything—even the painful stuff—was conveyed with her irrepressible sense of humor.

She told me a story I had never heard—that when she had come to New York with Neal in 1949, and then he turned around and wanted to drag her right back to the West Coast, she figured out a way to thwart him. She loved New York, and she was starting to love Jack Kerouac at that time, and she wanted to stay in the Big Apple at least a while longer. Ginsberg, too, didn't want Neal running off so fast. So she and Allen announced their plans to live together in New York, and Allen was going to "go straight." She let out a big laugh before she continued with the story. "Our real motive," she confided, "was to make Neal jealous, because he'd never want to lose Allen and me to each other! He'd be back east in two days if we ever really did that." The plan fell through, she said, only because Allen was less than keen about actually trying to become her lover.

Nick Nolte didn't seem anything like Neal to her. "Neal moved much faster than Nick Nolte," she said. "When I met Neal, he had six books under one arm, a pool cue in the other hand, and started necking with me at the same time."

A whole flood of memories came back to her; I was trying to take notes, but it was hard for me to keep up. Suddenly she was living back in those days—names of people were coming back to her hot and fast. She told me about three guys standing up at her wedding to Neal—Bill Tomson, Jim Holmes, and Jimmy Penoff. She was only 15, and her mom consented in order to get her out of the house, where Lu Anne was having a lot of problems with her stepfather and had become rebellious, more than her mom could handle.

She laughed about Bill Tomson, one of Neal's rivals in the local pool-hall gang, a guy who fancied himself as much a ladies' man as Neal. Bill wouldn't get out of their room on their wedding night; he wanted to share in the honeymoon. Again she laughed at one of her memories—how she had to kick Tomson out of the honeymoon suite, which was just a room Neal had rented in a private house, and where she worried that their noisy lovemaking that night kept the other residents up.

Lu Anne's eyes sparkled when she talked about Neal. She said Neal was always reading to her. She said he always wanted her back, that she didn't force herself on him, as Carolyn always claimed. Then she went into a reverie—she was thinking of Neal's letters, and her eyes got a little moist and unfocused. It was as if she left the hospital room with me for a few moments, her spirit traveling back decades and across a thousand miles of continent—as if she were being hit by waves of bittersweet pain, thinking of something that was once too beautiful, and way too beautiful to lose. "He wrote me the most marvelous love letters," she said finally. "It was when he had just come to San Francisco, and I was still in Denver, and he wanted me back in his life. He told me that he was a 'rudderless ship' without me, and other lovely things like that. The things he wrote overwhelmed me."

But it was the battle with Carolyn that obsessed her that afternoon in the hospital—a battle she had long ago lost, a defeat which the making of the movie now seemed to confirm and memorialize for all time. "Carolyn was a woman to me," Lu Anne pleaded for my sympathy. "What chance did I have? I was sixteen, and she was in her twenties. Carolyn's making herself look good in this movie. She portrays herself as this beautiful and sophisticated woman, this siren, that two brilliant and experienced men fell madly in love with. That's not the way it was at all. Carolyn had merely got herself pregnant."

She went after Carolyn in a way that I would learn was not characteristic of her. Lu Anne was usually the most forgiving of people. She was also known for being gracious. It may have been her current situation, being sick and helpless in a hospital bed while Carolyn romped with movie stars and ate at glamorous five-star restaurants down in Hollywood. Lu Anne was almost penniless at the time, though I didn't know it then. It may also have been, as her daughter later pointed out to me, the bad temper that sometimes accompanied Lu Anne's coming down off her many medications.

"Carolyn and Neal weren't making it together," Lu Anne said. "Only a short time after they got married, the sex had stopped. It was that simple. That's why he was so desperate to get me back."

We talked for a while more, until she started to tire. I was trying to get as much information as I could from her, but this wasn't the sort of full interview I had wanted. She didn't know when she would be out of the hospital, and I didn't have the money to stay in San Francisco much longer. I figured whatever I got from her that day was all I was going to get. She told me I'd have to go—she needed her rest.

"When you come back, I'll buy you lunch," she told me, batting her eyelashes at me. I couldn't believe it. She was flirting with me—mildly, it's true, but still flirting. "Then we can sit in the park and hold hands."

I was twenty years younger than she, but completely smitten. She was beautiful, she was clearly wounded, and she was unbelievably charming.

"Then we'll have something to look forward to," I said. I must have looked like a puppy dog in love.

She told me she needed some candy and a pack of Winstons, and I set off on the run for the commissary. It's kind of amazing to look back and remember that in the 1970s you could still buy cigarettes in a hospital—for all I know, they even had a lounge for patients where Lu Anne could have smoked them. In any case, I returned in a jiffy and handed her the Winstons and the three candy bars she'd requested.

"Thanks, honey," she said. I was rewarded by the warm, glowing smile of a well-loved woman. It was clear she was used to attention from men, and she still liked it. Something about her expression reminded me of a purring cat—the visual equivalent of a cat's purr.

I extended my hand to her. Still a Midwesterner, I was ready to part with a handshake. But she grabbed my hand with both her good hand and the bandaged one, and gave me a loving squeeze.

"Get well soon," I said, trying to convey a little burst of healing energy in her direction. I was no longer thinking of my much-sought interview. I just wanted her to be well, to be happy. The fact is, she had charmed the socks off me—no mean feat for a middle-aged woman with no makeup, a bandaged hand, and dressed in a baggy hospital gown. I left the room with her oodles of charisma trailing after me—feeling as if I had just been granted a meeting with Hedy Lamarr or Lana Turner.

Then, the next day, came yet another surprise. I got a call from Lu Anne. She was out of the hospital and staying with an old friend, Joe DeSanti, in Daly City. She wanted to do the full, taped interview I had talked of with her. A day or two later, when she was rested enough, I drove down to Joe's tract house in Daly City, carrying a shoulder bag full of notebooks, tapes, and recording equipment.

Daly City is a working-class suburb in the heavy-fog belt just south of San Francisco. The sky is always gray, and the small, single-story houses are grayish too and tend to be almost indistinguishable from one another. The town has always comprised a lot of immigrants and those who can't afford the pricey rents of the city itself. It is a bedroom community with few businesses and restaurants and no nightlife whatsoever. One didn't expect to find Marylou of *On the Road* there, even a recuperating Marylou just out of the hospital.

I spent almost eight hours with her there that day, and for most of that time she remained in a dark-colored, maybe green, overstuffed armchair. I had my tape recorder set in front of her, on a low, round, polished, middle-class coffee table. The furnishings were tasteful but sparse. The house did not look lived-in at all, and the only other resident was apparently Joe himself. There were large glass windows—a California trademark—but they were almost all covered with heavy drapes. Privacy seemed to be the word of the day here. The coffee table also held a large ashtray for her many cigarettes an hour.

Lu Anne looked puffy and unwell, and her voice was slow and not nearly as strong or energetic as it had been in the hospital a couple of days before. But I could see the strength and determination in her. She could easily have made a poor-health excuse and bowed out of the engagement, but she was determined to tell me everything she had to say, and she kept going even when I began to wear down myself. She kept going even though Joe frequently interrupted with hints that she quit for the day. At one point he even suggested that it was time for her to visit her daughter Annie Ree, who was living close by and raising her own baby now. Lu Anne brushed him off like a queen whose word is unchallengeable. She made it very clear to him how important it was for her to do this interview with me. In some ways, her sedulous insistence on getting her whole story told was an extension of the feelings she'd expressed earlier, in the hospital, about her horror at seeing her role in Beat history distorted and mistold in the movie *Heart Beat* and elsewhere. Having already been gravely ill several times, she now strongly feared that her real story would never get told correctly. And so she filled cassette tape after cassette tape with the interview I could hardly believe I was finally getting. And what an interview it was!

Listening to the tapes now more than 30 years later, I realized how much of what she'd said that day I had forgotten—and how much else had simply gone over my head, because I was not yet old enough, nor had I lived enough, to appreciate all the profound life lessons she was sharing with me. If there's anyone with more insight into Jack Kerouac and Neal Cassady than Lu Anne, I have yet to encounter them. I used to think John Clellon Holmes in his several essays, especially "The Great Rememberer," had the most profound insights into Kerouac. In some ways, perhaps, he still does. But he did not see the whole other dimension of Jack that a woman, especially a sensitive woman like Lu Anne, saw; and Holmes was not nearly as sharp or empathetic about Cassady.

Carolyn Cassady has now written and rewritten several memoirs, but to my mind they are more about her than they are about Neal and Jack. And Carolyn, not to put too fine a point on it, belonged for better or worse to the square world that Jack and Neal were always trying to run away from. She was more a friendly opponent than somebody who understood from the inside the world they inhabited.

But Lu Anne was unquestionably on the inside, and remained there even after spending decades exiled from the Beat world in the squaresville suburb of Daly City. Even amid the plethora of Beat interviews that now exist, Lu Anne's interview with me is a unique document, I think. Unlike so many of the other women who have written about Kerouac—including Joyce Johnson, Edie Parker Kerouac, and Helen Weaver—she resists the temptation to shift the focus of the story from Jack (or in this case, Jack and Neal) to herself. Through an almost seven-hour interview, Lu Anne stays on point about those two men, *the* American countercultural icons of the twentieth century. And she sees them with an objective accuracy that is uncanny, but also with a compassion and nonjudgmental attitude that is worthy of a bodhisattva—which, forgive my presumption, I would make the claim that she was.

Beat fans, who want the same shopworn but comforting portraits of their two favorite happy outlaws, the Butch Cassidy and Sundance Kid of the 1950s, need be prepared to go down the Rabbit Hole and through the Looking-Glass. For what they will find in Lu Anne's memoir are two men who may be almost unrecognizable to them—and certainly neither one of them are anything resembling an outlaw hero or even antihero. Kerouac may have written some of the greatest and most innovative books of the twentieth century, but Lu Anne portrays him as a man who couldn't go out and find a job to pay the rent when it was crunch time—a man who, when the pressures of the ordinary world built up too high, froze in his tracks and had to let a teenage girl show him the way forward.

Neal she shows to be a man of enormous vulnerability around both men and women—a man who would rather pimp his wives and girlfriends to other men than risk having them choose another lover on their own; a man who, when he finds another man, a large strong young man, kissing his wife, does nothing but scream and scream and then demand everyone in his party turn tail and flee. Cassady's male bravado, which became as much a symbol for the age as Brando's sneer, is revealed to be a mask for his own monumental uncertainty. Lu Anne shows Neal to be a man for whom decisions of any kind were inordinately hard; hence we see his endless crisscrossing of the country, San Francisco to Denver to San Francisco to New York and back to San Francisco, ad infinitum, to be less the intrepid travelings (to borrow a phrase from Neal's later master, Ken Kesey) of a New Age explorer, and more the futile and endless missteps of a man who could never truly figure any real direction for himself in life.

Lu Anne has routinely been portrayed as a teenage slut—a sex bomb without much of a mind, which is certainly how she came off in the movie *Heart Beat*. We could impute this chiefly to the imagination of salacious filmmakers—and maybe to the fantasy life of many prurient biographers and critics as well—except that now, with a wealth of Beat primary source material finally being made public, we see that a good many of the Beats, Kerouac included, did not feel much differently about her—at least when their sexual hormones were flowing. Wandering Denver by himself in 1949, as Kerouac writes to Ginsberg, he "thought any moment LuAnne would sneak up behind me and grab my cock." And after she visits him with Neal and Al Hinkle at his little Berkeley cottage in 1957— a scene Lu Anne relates in detail in the interview—Jack writes to Allen that "Neal and Al Hinkle floated into my Berkeley door just as I was unpacking boxful of *On The Roads* from Viking, all got high reading, LuAnne wanted to fuck me that next night...," which is not how she relates the incident at all.* To his credit, when Kerouac was one-on-one with Lu Anne in conversation, without any other males around to impress, and when his macho image was not at stake, she often found him a good listener and sympathetic friend.

Quite the opposite of the clichéd sex symbol or ditzy blonde, the Lu Anne we see in her interview is keenly observant, sensitive, and thoughtful not just about the lives of herself and her friends, but repeatedly about the human condition as well. One of the little pleasures of the piece is her attentiveness to how writers work. She describes John Clellon Holmes at his little typing table in the center of his busy Manhattan living room, and Alan Harrington plunked down at his typewriter in front of his little Indian hut, writing outdoors in the baking heat of the Arizona desert. If not for her powers of observation, we might not realize how unusual Kerouac's own writing style

---

* *Jack Kerouac and Allen Ginsberg: The Letters*, edited by Bill Morgan and David Stanford (New York: Viking, 2010), p. 108 and p. 352.

was, constantly scribbling in pencil in his nickel notebooks wherever he found himself, whether in a car, on foot, or just sitting with a cup of coffee in some lost café midway across the continent. It is those same powers of observation that force us to see Lu Anne herself from a different slant. Paired with Cassady, who comes off as the socio-pathic user of a young girl barely into her second year of high school, Lu Anne starts to look a lot more like an abused innocent. By the same token, Kerouac looks a lot less like the male chauvinist he's been typed as, especially by female critics; and his repeated concern for Lu Anne's well-being shows him to be a lot more compassionate and empathetic with women than most men of the day.

Despite the fact that Neal does such terrible things to her—forcing her to commit grand larceny and risk going to prison, at an age when most girls have no tougher decisions to make than what length of skirt to wear and which boy to go to the high school dance with—Lu Anne insists on seeing the good in Neal, and focuses on the purity of his heart and the grandeur of his mind, rather than his myriad bad deeds. Such vision is due not only to a special, almost saintlike largesse in her, but also to an extraordinary caring and concern for other people that seems to have been one of the lifelong trademarks of her character. We see Neal stomping through other people's homes and devouring their food—not to mention taking their money, when it slips too near to the gravitational pull of his vast hunger and neediness—whereas Lu Anne wouldn't think of staying at a strange woman's home, such as Jack's mother's, without sweeping the floor once a day and replenishing the food in the icebox with her own funds, even if it means pawning a prized watch and a gold engagement ring.

In many ways, Lu Anne was like the conscience Neal didn't have. That he kept coming back to her, even after he'd left all the other women in his life by the wayside or dead, speaks well for his own character, as if living without a conscience bothered him more than he ever let on. Lu Anne saw this too, and it is evident in the angry tirade she let loose near the end of the interview, where she railed against the many people, including his second wife, Carolyn, who considered Neal patently irresponsible.

Lu Anne had that rare ability to see people in their totality—their pluses and their minuses, their ups and downs, their ins and out— and to see each one as a whole person. Whatever Neal might do, she passed no judgment on him. She didn't see a good person or a bad person, but just, "This is Neal." In like manner, she had the ability to see what was precious in every person. It wasn't a Pollyannaish sort of blind optimism. She was quite aware of how flawed people were, but despite their flaws, she could also see that there was a beauty, a unique and lovely flame, in every human being. It was the pursuit of that flame that set her life on its amazing course. In her ability to see, and cherish, the inspirational power in men like Kerouac and Cassady, she herself became an inspirational force, and left her own lasting impression on some of the finest writers of her time.

In July 2010, just prior to the filming of *On the Road,* I was invited by director Walter Salles up to Montreal to serve as the first "drill instructor" at the Beat Boot Camp he had set up for his actors. It was my job to somehow make these twentysomething kids (as they seemed to me) understand the essence of each of their characters. Kristen Stewart, who was about to play Lu Anne in the movie, was having a hard time making sense of how Lu Anne could still love Neal, despite his endless cheating on her. She had just learned that Lu Anne continued seeing Neal in later years, and she asked me, "How was she finally able to leave him? And what happened afterward?" She wondered if Lu Anne were just so stupid that she remained Neal's dupe for much of her life; and if so, when did she finally figure out that she was being played for a fool?

Marie Lussier-Timperley, Kristen Stewart, and J. A. Michel Bornais, Montreal, July 2010. Lussier-Timperley and Bornais are relatives of Jack Kerouac. (Photo by Gerald Nicosia.)

I asked Kristen to turn that perspective around, and to see that Lu Anne was continually making her own choices to be with this man, to love him, to learn from him, and to give him the things he so desperately needed, starting with the tenderness he had been denied since growing up motherless, and with a dysfunctional wino father, on the skid row streets of Denver. I suggested to her that it was Lu Anne who actually taught Neal and Jack how to love each other. Later, listening to my taped interview with Lu Anne, Kristen said she found the key to playing Marylou in the movie was to see her "as her own woman, not Neal's." She would later tell Annie Santos, Lu Anne's daughter, who also traveled to Montreal to coach the actors, that she'd come to see Lu Anne as the energy source for both men, and for *On the Road* itself. In Kristen's words, "Jack and Neal needed that estrogen." Kristen had gotten it—or *it*, as Neal might have said—better than I'd hoped.

But back to that puffy, pale, unwell 48-year-old woman in the Daly City living room. I couldn't help thinking it must have been a strange journey that led her from a middle-class home in provincial 1940s Denver to hang with the wildest hipsters in New York City and San Francisco, digging jazz, free sex, and every sort of drug available—and then back again to the most conventional milieu this side of *Ozzie and Harriet.* Yet she never entirely lost her naïve quality; touches of that charming innocence remained, even during our interview, as when she wonders over the fact that she could recall so little of what happened after she and the boys smoked opium together after John Holmes's big New Year's Eve party.

A lot of Lu Anne was beyond me then, due to my own inexperience and the limits to my understanding imposed by a Catholic, middle-class upbringing. I only knew how grateful I was for the interview, and I sensed how great it was, though I would not grasp until quite recently how much Lu Anne had given me that day— how much of herself she had shared. The interview had been locked up for many years in a university archive until recently freed by a lawsuit I was forced to bring—but that's a matter for another story, only barely tangential to this one. Even after the interview was once again released to my custody, it lay buried away until Walter Salles coaxed me to bring it along up to Montreal to help Kristen better inhabit her part in the movie. Listening to it just before I left California, and then again with the actors in Montreal, I was finally blown away by its incredible power—the depth of Lu Anne's insights and the stunning revelations that she made so offhandedly they might have been cups of coffee she was handing me during the interview. I was reminded of how Picasso's painting *Les Demoiselles d'Avignon* had lain gathering dust, unwanted and unviewed, in his Parisian studio for seven and a half years, until someone noticed it and asked him to put it in a show, and then it proceeded to stand the twentieth-century art world on its head.

My point here is that I was not prepared to ask Lu Anne what had happened to her, nor did I feel I had the right. Clues would come to me only slowly, in small installments, over the years. I remember one such clue came in a story Al Hinkle told me, about how Neal came to him right after he'd met Lu Anne, brimming with the sort of excitement, not to say bald-faced lust, that only a new, beautiful woman could inspire in him.

"I just found the perfect woman!" Neal told Al. "She's got absolutely everything I always wanted."

Al recalled how a dark cloud suddenly passed across Neal's face.

"So what's the matter, then?" Al asked.

"The only trouble with her," Neal said, "is she's too much like me."

He had found his female equivalent, and he knew it would be trouble for both of them, and indeed it was.

I did get one clue that day, however. As I packed up my tapes and recording equipment, Lu Anne approached me with a worried look on her face.

"I have to ask a favor of you," she said. At that point I would likely have done anything she asked, but she seemed anxious about the request she was about to make. I also thought I sensed a little fear in her face—I wasn't sure what of. Perhaps fear that I would turn her down.

"I have to have twenty dollars," she said. "Can you give me that much?"

Twenty dollars was a lot more in 1978 than it is today, and I was traveling on a pretty thin margin in those days. But I handed her the twenty without question, nor did either of us say anything about paying it back. For my part, I figured she'd earned it by all the work she'd done that day talking into my tape recorder. I didn't feel used or taken advantage of. If anyone had been leaning on another's good will, it had been me leaning on her for an interview that was going to help me put my book over the top.

I was curious about it, though. I brought it up with Larry Lee before I left California.

"She acted almost desperate for that money," I told Larry. "Do you have any idea what's going on with her?"

Just as he knew everyone, Larry also knew the dirt, the lowdown, on the life of everybody he dealt with. I don't know how he knew it, but good journalists do that. It's part of their job. And Larry was one of the best journalists there ever was.

"She needed the money for a fix," Larry said. "She's a junkie."

And he left me to mull that over all the way back to Chicago.

Note to the Transcription

—————⬥—————

Turning transcribed interviews into a readable text is a fine art. In this case, I was working with two different interviews, one that I had taken down in handwriting in a notebook, and another that I had taped and then transcribed on a typewriter. The pitfalls are many. Most verbatim interviews are barely readable—broken syntax, too many false starts, repetitions, thoughts left hanging and picked up many pages later. The editor has to "clean up" the interview, but there is a great danger in overcleaning. There is a tendency to correct all incorrect grammar, to replace all slangy expressions with higher-class vocabulary words, and so forth. On the other hand, a reader stumbling through a too-faithful rendition of the words out of an interviewee's mouth can lose patience very quickly and feel that the text is not worth the trouble of reading, let alone trying to understand.

When the interviewee is dead, as Lu Anne now is, there is an even heavier responsibility to try to keep the exactness of her meaning, since she isn't around to correct the misrepresentation of it. I tried to err on the side of fidelity, rather than on the side of a suave-sounding text. But there was something more going on as I tried to render those tens of thousands of taped words into a coherent, readable narrative. Lu Anne had little formal education, but her language had its own flavor, its own homespun charm, much like the tinge of western accent with which she spoke. I tried very hard to keep the sound of her voice in the printed interview. She had a way of repeating certain words for emphasis—"a beautiful, beautiful house," for example— that was very typical of her speech patterns. That sort of repetition tends to get cut immediately by editors, but I left most such instances in, because it was a unique signature of her speech and, even more importantly, part of the way she thought. She was excitable; she was filled with enthusiasm—those were things Jack Kerouac and others loved about her. That enthusiasm showed up so clearly in her doubling of words—as well as in the frequent "My Gods," a smattering of which I also left in. Furthermore, I chose to keep solecisms like "we laid in the grass," "he was gonna write," and such incorrect but common usages as "I could've cared less"—because this is the way she talked. She didn't sound like a high-society lady, and I didn't intend to make her sound like one.

Another reason I was hesitant to excise too much, even of her repetitions, was that she tended to think aloud as she was talking, to think things through even as she was recalling them to me; and it was clear she was learning new things about her life even as she purported simply to tell me what had happened to her over the years. I wanted the reader of this interview to get that sense of her thinking aloud and following her own thoughts down new and unknown trails. To some extent, I did follow the normal procedure in redacting an interview, bringing together passages on the same subject that might appear at different points in the conversation. Interviewees often start to talk about a subject, then go off to something else, then return to the first subject when some new thought or memory strikes them about what they had been saying previously. It can be too disruptive to the reader to print accounts of various events broken up the way that people actually remember and speak them. So, for example, when Lu Anne tells of her trip from Denver to North Carolina with Neal and Al Hinkle in December 1948, I meld the several incomplete versions of the trip she gave at different points in the taped interview. But there were several places where I chose to go with a much more faithful rendition of the actual flow of her speech.

One of the charms of listening to Lu Anne was the pleasure of watching the associative trains, and occasional leaps, of her thoughts—the way one memory triggered another somewhat deeper, and then another deeper still, or the way she would sometimes keep getting pulled back to retell a story by the insistent demands of feelings that had not yet gotten fully expressed. An example of the former process is how, early in the taped interview, when she is talking about meeting Jack Kerouac and being puzzled by how shy he was in approaching girls, her mind suddenly jumps ahead a couple of years to the infamous New Year's Eve party chronicled in both *On the Road* and John Clellon Holmes's novel *Go*. She uses an event at that party to drive home her point about Jack's inability to be subtle with women, and his bitterness about his own ineptitude. Since she talked at length later on about that party, the traditional approach would have been to cut the party scene from the chronicle of late 1946, where it didn't belong, and move it up to the passages about late 1948 / early 1949. But you learn a lot about Jack quickly by getting to that party scene early, and you also learn a lot about the way Lu Anne's mind works in her remembering of it—so I left the flow there just as it came from her lips.

The latter reason for keeping the flow intact, the fact that she could not resist trying and trying again to get a story told right, until her own feelings were satisfied, is shown most strongly in the section of the interview where she relates how Neal, after a wonderfully companionable trip across the country together in Neal's brand-new Hudson in early 1949, coldly and callously abandons Lu Anne and Jack on a street corner in San Francisco. I retained the order of her thoughts in that long section exactly as they were recorded on the tape. In some ways, that section is the climax of the interview, just as Jack used that scene for the climactic moment in *On the Road*. Lu Anne tells how hurt Jack was by Neal's deserting them, and how the incident merely reinforced her own knowledge and acceptance of Neal's ability to inflict hurt; but then Lu Anne circles back to it, retells it with more detail, begins to focus more on the fact that she and Jack talked of getting married, revisits it again and reveals something she says she has told no one else, that Jack cried in her arms that first night at the Blackstone Hotel, and then, finally, comes back to it again and begins to muse on the prospect that, had the facts of the situation been only a little different, she and Jack might have ended up happily married and gone on to lead entirely different lives than the tragic and unfulfilled ones they did live.

I thought it was essential that the reader see—that is, listen to— Lu Anne going back again and again to that episode, as its impact and ramifications began to strike her with greater and greater force, *as she let it sink into her own conscious mind*, and allowed herself to understand what had really happened between her and Jack at that time. There is no question—after hearing Lu Anne's account— that she and Jack had both reached a critical point in their lives during the two weeks they spent at the Blackstone Hotel. There can also be no doubt that, had she married Jack, her subsequent life would have been vastly different—perhaps not easier, but certainly less disjointed, less disconnected, and filled with a far greater satisfaction of her emotional needs, and perhaps a far greater flowering of her own gifts.

For Jack, it would have meant marriage to a woman who truly loved him, and he would have been saved from the debacle of that impromptu marriage to Joan Haverty a year and a half later, born far more of his desperation to put his life in order than from any kind of real love or even respect between them. Jan Kerouac would never have been born, to live out her life with two uncaring parents, or maybe she would have been born in a different body—if you believe in reincarnation—to Jack and Lu Anne. But now we're in the realm of speculation. To return to facts, it's pretty evident that Jack's iron-fisted Catholic mother, Mémère, would never have allowed him to marry "that type of woman"—for Lu Anne would have seemed like the worst kind of tramp to her narrow-minded morality.

In any case, it's interesting to see that Kerouac himself felt the critical importance of that juncture in his life, just as Lu Anne did. In a scene from *On the Road* that he told Allen Ginsberg was the most important in the book, just after Neal abandons Jack and Lu Anne (Sal and Marylou), Sal wanders the streets of San Francisco penniless, picking up cigarette butts from the pavement, and suddenly imagines that a woman in a fish-and-chips joint on Market Street gives him a "terrified look," as if she sees their past lives together two hundred years earlier, when Sal is her thieving son just returned from jail. "I stopped, frozen in ecstasy on the sidewalk," Kerouac writes, and then goes on for two more pages of the most dazzling, poetic and metaphysical prose he ever wrote, describing "the plank where all the angels dove off and flew into the holy void of uncreated emptiness," and on and on and on, leaving the reader dizzy and exhausted at the end of a literary ride like no other I can think of.*

---

* *On the Road* (New York: Penguin paperback edition, 1991), pp. 172–174.

There is nothing in the novel about Jack considering getting married to Lu Anne, or about crying in her arms, but he could not have come up with any more powerful metaphor for the emotional trauma and transformations he was going through at that moment.

One more point needs mentioning briefly. Besides the fact that the second and longer interview I did with Lu Anne, which was taped, provides a far more accurate rendering of her words than the notes I took in longhand (though one can mishear words on a tape too), there is the additional problem that the tone of the two interviews differs a great deal. In the hospital, not sure how much of what she was saying was "on the record," Lu Anne was a lot franker with me about many things, including her feelings about Carolyn Cassady; and she was also, because of her helpless situation—penniless in a hospital bed while others seemed to be making hay off the Beat life she'd led—a lot angrier than when she was safely ensconced back in her friend Joe's house. Her language in the hospital was in general a lot rawer and more uncensored. On tape, she was milder in what she said about Carolyn, only once throwing a mild jab at her, where she says that after Neal broke his thumb he "ran back to his mother," meaning Carolyn and implying the essentially nonsexual relationship between them that she had spelled out for me in the hospital. Although I chose to blend some accounts from the hospital with the same events narrated on the tape, I chose to keep others separate, to avoid creating a jarring shift in the tone. Thus I saved much of what she said about Carolyn for the introduction to this book. I also felt certain things, such as Lu Anne's reactions to the filming of *Heart Beat*, needed to be kept discrete from the main text of the interview. Hence they are now also part of the introduction instead.

Gerald Nicosia
January 18, 2011

Lu Anne, World War II pinup, taken by her stepfather, Steve Henderson, 1944. (Photo courtesy of Anne Marie Santos.)

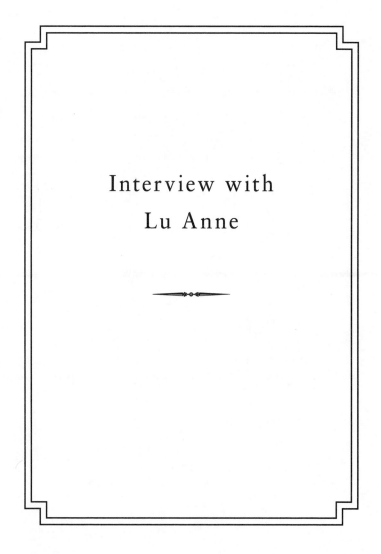

Interview with
Lu Anne

INTERVIEW WITH LU ANNE

PART ONE

B y the end of 1946, Jack Kerouac had lived for nearly seven
years in New York, seven years that were as intensely lived
*and filled with incident as 77 years in another man's life—in short,
he already had a whole private history there. He had come from
Lowell, Massachusetts, a depressed mill town, "Stinktown on the
Merrimac" his father had called it. At 17—his head filled with
Thomas Wolfe and Jack London—he had been desperate to get out,
to go live somewhere where he could become a writer. His family
were poor Canucks, but his ticket out was his tremendous athletic
ability. He was, by all accounts, one of the best running backs
who had been seen in New England high school football—virtually unstoppable once he took off. He won a football scholarship
to Columbia University; but since his Lowell high school education
had been so spotty, they insisted he go to Horace Mann prep school
for a year, to bring him up to speed for college work. He started at
Horace Mann in the fall of 1939—just as the world was going to
war, he would later note ruefully.*

At first, though, he paid no attention to the war. He was too busy listening to jazz, both the big-band swing of Benny Goodman and Artie Shaw that was then in vogue, and also the underground birth of bebop in the little after-hours Harlem clubs, where he was led by a hip Jewish kid from Horace Mann named Seymour Wyse. Once he got to Columbia, his interest in jazz continued to grow, and he'd spend much of his time in his room reading Dostoyevsky and other great books he loved. He played little football, because Coach Lou Little (Luigi Piccolo) had a different favorite running back, an Italian named Paul Governali, and Kerouac's breaking a leg on the playing field didn't help things.

Jack Kerouac running for a touchdown for Lowell High School, fall of 1938. (Photographer unknown.)

But soon studies began to matter little to him, anyway, because he was plunging rapidly into a heady subculture of New York artistic intelligentsia, which included his future wife Edie Parker, an art student; piano-playing pre-law student Tom Livornese; would-be writers such as Allen Ginsberg and Lucien Carr; creative and unconventional college students such as Hal Chase (anthropology) and Ed White (architecture); and bookish petty criminals such as William Burroughs and Herbert Huncke. This offbeat group (pardon the pun) enjoyed the fleshly kicks of booze, drugs, and sex as much as they enjoyed high-level, soul-searching rap sessions, since they were for the most part a troubled bunch of young people—some of them actual outcasts from society and their disapproving families, and some of them just feeling outcast in a world that now worshipped power in the form of atom bombs and commercial success in the form of look-alike tract houses and gray flannel suits.

In 1942, Kerouac dropped out of Columbia completely. He got kicked out of the Navy because he laid down his rifle on the drill field, announcing that he didn't want to kill anyone. He still wanted to serve his country, however, and did so in the Merchant Marine, sailing on the famed S.S. Dorchester the run before it was torpedoed by a German U-boat, resulting in the loss of nearly 700 lives. Kerouac remained patriotic all his life, but when he returned permanently to New York after yet another dangerous merchant voyage, he was embittered and feeling let down by society in general. When Carr stabbed a man to death one night in Morningside Heights, Kerouac helped him dispose of the knife and other evidence, ready to become a criminal himself. He had decided that society's rules were at best meaningless, if not downright destructive, and that friendship was really the only thing that mattered.

After the war and America's so-called victory, which had come at the price of millions of deaths, Kerouac and his friends were all the more convinced that society's values were bankrupt, and that some kind of new personal code had to be forged. They knew it was the role of the artist to create those new values; but they could no longer figure out what, if any, role the artist and writer might have in modern society, which seemed bent on stamping out individuality in all forms, and seemed to view different behavior of any kind as a red flag of warning.

Kerouac and Ginsberg, especially, discussed, argued, and pondered what they should do with their lives, what and how they should write, what their proper subjects should be, and so forth— endlessly, in late-night discussions in 24-hour diners and unkempt hipster flats, and in literally hundreds of letters back and forth. Many of these letters have recently been published, and they are often stunningly brilliant, but they also show two young proto- geniuses who have reached an absolute dead end. They comment ad infinitum on books they have read, each other's writings, and every little incident in their rather tame if sordid lives—but they get nowhere. They reach no resolution. They are looking for a way out and cannot find it.*

And then the answer came to them, in the form of a wild man from Denver blazing across the plains in a stolen car—and later, when the car broke down from being pushed too hard, a Grey- hound bus—with his drop-dead-beautiful 16-year-old wife and volumes of Proust and Shakespeare in his small, battered suitcase. The man was 20-year-old Neal Cassady, and his wife was Lu Anne Henderson, whose greatest adventure until recently had been drinking a few beers and smoking a little pot with Neal and his guy

---

* *Jack Kerouac and Allen Ginsberg: The Letters,* edited by Bill Morgan and David Stanford (New York: Viking Press, 2010).

Neal Cassady, San Francisco, circa 1948. (Courtesy of Carolyn Cassady.)

friends and a bunch of other giggling high school girls at a vacant house in the Rocky Mountains just above Denver.

Neal Cassady, however, had lived pretty hard before marrying Lu Anne and dragging her off to New York to fulfill his lifelong dream of becoming a famous writer. (He'd already given up the dream of playing left end for Notre Dame.) Abandoned by his mother when he was six—in 1932, the depths of the Great Depression—Neal went to live with his barber father, a far-gone wino, on Larimer Street, the skid row of Denver. He was a sweet kid, a Catholic choir boy for a while, very bright as well as good-looking and athletic. He did his best at school and tried to keep his perpetually drunken father out of trouble. But he was also one of the most highly sexed males on the planet and couldn't keep his hands off female bodies. By his own account, he began sex play with little girls when he was eight, and by the time he was 12 was having sexual intercourse regularly with both girls and grown women.

It wasn't easy for a kid on skid row to find places to have sex, so at 14 Neal began stealing cars—joyriding it was called then— where he'd grab a car with the keys left in the ignition, or hotwire a car, go pick up his latest girl, whirl her up to the mountains for a quickie in one of those empty houses or cabins he knew so well, and try to get the car back before anyone noticed it missing. He later claimed to have stolen about 500 cars while still in his teens. The problem was that people did notice their cars missing, and Neal was arrested many times. He spent his youth in and out of reform schools, most memorably (and excruciatingly) at the Colorado State Reformatory at Buena Vista, an institution nearly as brutal as an adult penitentiary.

Between skid row and jail, Neal learned that he could enjoy sex with males too. He always preferred his erotic pleasures with women, but men had one distinct advantage: they were usually willing to pay him for the privilege of a roll in the hay. Before he was incarcerated at Buena Vista, he had worked as a male hustler in Denver. One day he ran across a very powerful gay lawyer and high school counselor named Justin Brierly, who also served as an admissions advisor to his alma mater, Columbia University. Brierly often arranged for his favorite young men, if they were bright enough, to get accepted at Columbia. Brierly was totally smitten with Cassady, and there was no doubt that with his 132 IQ (which Brierly got tested for him) Neal was smart enough to handle college studies. But of course it was not going to be easy, Brierly knew, to get a high school dropout with a long criminal record into an Ivy League school.

Lu Anne, about age 13, and Dorie (wife of Lu Anne's half brother Lloyd) in the Rocky Mountains of Colorado. (Photo courtesy of Anne Marie Santos.)

Brierly took the tack of introducing Cassady to some of the other young men whom he had helped to become successful students at Columbia, a group that included Hal Chase and Ed White. After corresponding for several months with Neal while he was in prison—and being highly impressed by Neal's letter-writing ability—Chase met Cassady in person and became close friends with him. Chase also talked about Cassady, and showed Neal's letters around, to his own gang at Columbia, including Kerouac and Ginsberg, who were quite intrigued. Chase went so far as to set up special oral examinations for Cassady with several Columbia professors—with the promise that, if he passed, he would be allowed to matriculate there. The exams were supposed to take place in September 1946; but in typical Cassady form, he didn't show up to take them.

Lu Anne, age 13, in Rocky Mountains near Peetz, Colorado, where her family lived. (Photo courtesy of Anne Marie Santos.)

He did have an excuse, however. Earlier in the year, he had walked into the Walgreens drugstore on 16th Street in Denver with his pool hall buddy Jimmy Holmes and his current girlfriend, Jeannie Stewart, and spotted two girls he didn't know talking in a booth. One of the girls, the blonde, captured his heart and his imagination the instant he saw her. Neal never explained what impressed him so much—if it were her looks, her animated manner, or the sunshine that almost everyone claimed radiated from her face. In any case, he leaned over to Holmes and whispered, "I'm gonna marry that girl. I don't know her, but she's my ideal—the girl I want to spend my life with." Jeannie said she knew both the girls from school—their names were Lois and Lu Anne. Neal suggested that the blonde, Lu Anne, would make a great date for their mutual friend Dickie Reed at a party they were about to have up in the mountains. Neal casually asked Jeannie to go over and get Lu Anne's phone number; and Jeannie, unaware of the treachery, went over and did as he asked.

Three weeks later, Neal did indeed marry Lu Anne. He had no place to live with his new bride, however, nor did Jeannie want to let loose of him. Finding his life far more complicated than he'd ever imagined it could be, by the fall of 1946 Neal had a lot more on his mind than going to college.

Lu Anne:

It all started in October 1946. That's when we took our first trip to New York. Neal and I sort of ran off from Denver because of what happened between Neal and a girl named Jeannie Stewart. She was this girl Neal had been living with when Neal and I met, and she was holding his clothes as a weapon to get him to come back "where he belonged." She wanted to keep him at her house, and he told her that he wasn't going to do that. So Neal and I went to her house, and he climbed up three stories and broke in the window, and rescued his clothes and books. His books were the most important thing to him at the time.

We ran off without anyone even knowing, just took off hitch-hiking, and we wound up in Sidney, Nebraska, where I had an aunt and uncle living. In Sidney, Neal got a job as a dishwasher, and I got a job as a maid—making twelve dollars a month! When I think back, my God! What child slavery they practiced in those days! They really did. One day off a month—that's all I got. I had to be up at five in the morning and have the whole bottom part of the house cleaned by the time the family got up at seven, and I finished at seven in the evening. But it all came to an abrupt end very soon.

It was just getting into winter, and we were having our second snow already. The woman, Mrs. Moore, had me out on this veranda scrubbing everything—the railings, even the side of the house. Neal happened to come home that day and saw me scrubbing this idiot thing—he saw that my hands were turning blue. He said, "That's it!" So that's when he took my uncle's car. He just told me he was gonna get a car—he didn't tell me where he was gonna get it or anything. I almost died when he drove up in front, thinking what I would have to face with the family. But, in any case, we took off at midnight.

I only had one trunk, and we loaded it into the car. It was a wild ride, let me tell you, because the whole windshield was completely iced over, and the windshield wipers wouldn't work! And of course, Neal always had a terrible fear of the police, so he had me looking out the rear window to see if we were being chased. Since my uncle worked at the railroad, Neal had no idea when he might discover it and turn it over to the police. My uncle would have had no way of knowing it was Neal and I who had taken his car. Whether that would have made any difference in his going to the police I don't really know. In any case, Neal wound up on the passenger side, driving with his left hand, looking out the window with this scarf tied around his head, and me looking out the driver's side because all the windows were totally iced up—to see if anyone was following.

I'd never gone through anything like that in my life. My father was a policeman, and I'd grown up with policemen. I had no fear of

James Bullard, Lu Anne's dad, and Lu Anne, age 12, Compton, California, 1942. (Photo courtesy of Anne Marie Santos.)

policemen at all. They were part of me, you might say. But between Neal's fright of the police and my own fright of my uncle—my fear of being found out by the family, that I would have done such a thing—we were both pretty much out of our heads. We drove the car off the road a few times, and finally it went completely off the road, and he couldn't get it started again. We'd made it to another small town in Nebraska—I can't remember the name—but not too damn far from where we'd started. Maybe a hundred miles or so. It seemed like we'd been driving for hours—most of the night. We had intended to drive to this friend of Neal's, Ed Uhl, whose family had a ranch near Sterling, Colorado. Neal told me we were gonna go to Ed's and stay the night, and then have Ed drive us to Denver. We really had no idea at that point that we would end up in New York.

Of course, through the months we had talked over and over about Neal's big dream, which was to get to New York and take extension courses or whatever he had to do—anything—just so he could go to Columbia. Hal Chase and some of his other friends were already there. Neal didn't have a high school diploma, but Hal was supposedly setting up some kind of oral examinations so that Neal could get directly into Columbia anyway. Neal had talked so much about it, and we both dreamed about it; but like I said, up to that point we really hadn't made any definite plans.

When we'd left that night, we'd stolen some money. These people that I worked for had a box that they kept petty cash in; and when we left, Neal sent me upstairs to get it. It turned out there was close to three hundred dollars in it. To us, it seemed like a hell of a lot of money. So when the car went off the road, Neal said to me, very determined, "We're going to New York!" It turned out he'd been driving east all the while—the opposite of the way he would have needed to go to get to Ed Uhl's ranch. We were just outside of North

Platte, Nebraska. So we managed to get into North Platte and went straight to the bus station. We were both so excited just by the thought of it!

We didn't plan—we didn't anything! We just bought our tickets. *It was New York, you know—we couldn't wait!* Five days it took us on the bus, and of course Neal was so excited he couldn't sleep. He couldn't do anything except talk the whole way across about what we were going to do. We talked about this and that—but above all, he said *he was going to Columbia!* Suddenly we actually were making a million and one plans. When you're that age, everything is glorious and the world is yours. And one thing we had in our favor, money never bothered Neal and I. I mean, we were both average kids; we both liked nice clothes, and we both liked to have a good time. Of course, the raising Neal had, he'd had next to nothing. But I had been raised in what would be considered—especially for that period—a middle-class home. I'd had more than a few advantages, but it didn't bother me to give them up. We didn't mind being cold—we didn't mind anything! Really, we were happy just as long as we could go where we wanted to.

So when we got on the bus, then he told me all these fantastic things that he was gonna do. *He was gonna write*—that was his chief goal. And of course at this time too he was kind of going through a Pygmalion type of thing. And you've got to understand, with me—especially around Neal—I've always felt so inadequate, because I had never read any of these things that he was into. Proust and Shakespeare were the main writers he liked back then. Of course, I wanted to read them too, but I didn't know anything about them—about what books I should be reading. Neal was fantastic—like, when we were in Nebraska, we'd stay awake three-quarters of the night, and he would read Shakespeare to me. He was very patient as a teacher; he was reading to me constantly, or giving me books to read. If I didn't understand why they were important, he would sit down with me and we'd discuss them.

Neal was four years older than I was. I was fifteen when we married, but I was sixteen when we went to New York. All we did all the way across country was talk and read, and talk and read, and talk and read! When we got to New York, the first thing that happened was we got in a big fight in the bus station. I was going home, and I walked off. Of course, he came after me. We were both broke. Having no sense about money whatsoever, we had exactly thirty-five dollars in our pocket when we got there.

The first thing we did in New York was to go in a big cafeteria around the corner from the bus station. It was full of glittering foods, as Jack wrote, and it became a symbol of New York for Neal. When we walked in, neither one of us had ever seen anything like it. It was really just an automat, but we had never seen anything like all these goodies. Neal was always very magnanimous whenever he had anything in his pocket at all, just anything, so we were buying just about everything we saw. As I said, we had no sense about money.

Then, for what seemed like hours, we stood on Times Square looking at those big lighted signs. There was the Camel sign with someone blowing smoke rings; the black washerwoman, a typical mammy with a bandanna tied around her head, bending over this tub that suds came down from; and then there was Felix the Cat, acting out a series of little comic strips. These were all in neon lights that ran around the side of the Times Building. Neal and I used to talk about it years later. We must have stood there for at least three hours just enthralled looking at all of these things, the Times Building and all the neon signs. And then there were the Nesbitt's Orange stands, which were famous for their orange juice. We stopped in there, and it was the first time either of us had ever tasted an Orange Julius.

We started looking for a hotel, and none of them would rent us a room, because they thought we were trying to shack up. I didn't have our marriage license, and no one would believe us. No one would rent us a room. In one hotel, somewhere right near Times Square, there was a long stairway with a desk at the top, and for some reason there was a policeman up there. I don't know whether it was a house of prostitution that had been raided, but something obviously had happened not too long beforehand. And the cop was pretty nice. When we walked up and Neal told him we wanted a room, the cop told him, "Why don't you just go find the back of a car or something?" You know, in other words, "You kids go shack up somewhere else, but don't be trying to rent hotel rooms around here." By this time, Neal was getting very irritated, he was just very upset, and he blew it.

Neal finally decided to try the St. George Hotel by himself. He said, "You wait downstairs," and he went up and rented a single room. About an hour later, he came back down, and we got something to eat. Then he sneaked me up. I had to sneak up to get in the damned hotel, and our room was just a little tiny thing with a single bed in it, not even a double bed. Our window overlooked this alley—the world's worst impression of New York City your first night there! But to us it was beautiful. We lay there looking out the window all night long, with Neal telling me all of his little dreams and hopes for our future and what was going to happen in the days ahead. He was so excited and so full of ambition!

The next morning, we went up to Columbia University and looked up Neal's friends Hal Chase and Ed White. We hadn't met Allen Ginsberg yet. Neal was very, very fond of Hal, and very close to him, and Hal introduced us to Allen the first day. So right away we moved to a boys' dorm at Columbia, Livingston Hall. In the lobby there were all these couches and chairs, and we stayed there all day and half the night. Of course only Neal was allowed to go up to the rooms. But once, when they weren't watching too closely, Neal sneaked me up into one of the fellas' rooms.

I remember meeting Tom Livornese. He had dark, curly hair, and was a little more quiet than the others. He later said that all the guys were crazy about me, but I used to always feel so inadequate around all of them. In the first place, they were all so much older, and they all seemed so sophisticated, and so intelligent. I always felt like such a klutz around them. I loved every one of them, and I loved being around everything that was going on. They kind of treated me like one of the fellas—they really did! It wasn't like any of them was trying to get me off into a corner—nothing like that—because they were all very involved with each other and the happenings of the day. There weren't many women around, either—not that they weren't looking at all times, when we'd go into the bars and things like that. But I was usually the only girl that was around, because Neal had to spend ninety-nine percent of his time with the guys, and of course I was lost without Neal. I was scared to death to be alone there, anyway.

It wasn't long before I met Jack Kerouac too. Jack was on the quiet side, like Tom—at least at that time. He really wasn't an extrovert like a lot of the guys. Most of the guys were saying, "Yeah, come on! Let's go here! Let's go there!" Hal was kind of in between—he wasn't a total extrovert, but I wouldn't call him quiet and reserved, the way Jack was. It always seemed if you were alone talking to Jack, or if you were on a one-to-one basis with him, he was interested in what you said, and always acted very nice. I adored Jack anyway because he always treated me terrific! I never felt quite so inadequate around Jack—he just had that knack. He never talked down to me—*never!*

But when there was a group of people, Jack more or less listened. He was not one of the more active participants in all the conversations that were going on. Allen did a lot of the talking, but no one talked as much as Neal.

It seems like I met Jack on our first full day in New York. I'm almost certain it was in that dormitory at Columbia, and not the way he described it in *On the Road*. He wrote about Neal opening the door in the nude, but that didn't take place—at least when we first met Jack. There were several things in *On the Road*, actually lots and lots of little things, that Jack changed or just invented. That was one of the reasons he didn't want us to read the book, but I'll talk more about that later.

When we met Jack at Livingston Hall, several of the fellas were already there—five or six of them. Allen was there, probably Ed White too—I don't remember who all. And then Jack happened to walk in. Well, Allen had been telling Neal that he wanted him to meet Jack, and then all of a sudden: "This is Jack Kerouac!" And of course when Jack came in, especially in those days, any girl couldn't help looking at him. Jack commanded attention from the female because he was so pretty. He really was a handsome, handsome boy.

And of course Neal was immediately aware of it, which I think sort of attracted and repelled him at the same time. In a way, that was Neal's and Jack's immediate reaction to one another, because they both had mixed feelings about the other.

Jack appealed to Neal physically, and he was jealous automatically—tremendously jealous—of these beautiful looks of Jack. And after we were introduced, Neal was immediately drawn to him from his conversation. Jack never came on to girls—he never used his looks. In fact, it was like he was totally unaware of his own sex appeal. Really, it used to kind of amaze me. Jack never seemed to be aware of this attraction that he had for the female. In fact, it always seemed like he felt inadequate, like he wasn't much of a ladies' man. He would always say that the rest of the fellas could all do much

Jack Kerouac doing Bogart impression, New York, 1942.
(Courtesy of Edith Parker Kerouac.)

better than he could—he really always had that feeling, and he actually gave that impression. I really believe it to be so. I don't really think he had any egotism whatsoever concerning himself.

I later heard that Hal felt the same way—that it seemed strange to Hal too that Jack could never seem to get started with a girl. He always had to have an introduction from somebody, his friend's girlfriend or something, because he couldn't seem to make it on his own with girls. I don't think Jack had any confidence, which is really strange in a boy that looks like him. Especially in those days, a football player had no trouble finding a girlfriend. I don't care if you looked like Dracula, if you were on the football team, ninety percent of the girls in school were all over you! Just the prestige of the whole thing was a magnet for girls. But Jack, like I said, always seemed totally unaware of his own power as a male. He was never aggressive with women. I never saw Jack, unless with Neal's pushing him and maybe being loaded, get a little confidence to approach a girl. He'd finally get nerve enough, whatever you want to call it, but then he would overdo it—he would come on so strong and so bad that he'd scare the girl off!

I remember that party that John Clellon Holmes wrote about in his novel *Go*. This was a couple of years later, in 1948. It was this fantastic party that we went to on New Year's Eve in a huge basement apartment not too far from Columbia. I really didn't appreciate it at the time, not until I got older and realized how many different people were there—from Neal and I and all the fellas at Columbia to all sorts of out-of-town people, women from uptown, women with furs that I thought of as "older women," though they might only have been twenty-three or twenty-four years old. But they seemed very old and sophisticated to me, and it wasn't till years later that I realized how special a party it really was—and I wish I had been old enough to have been able to circulate a little bit. Because, we mostly stayed in one room with our own little group. Jack was loaded, and there was some girl there that Jack kind of had eyes for, and Neal was gonna fix the whole thing up. Well, Neal wound up going out to the car with her instead, and Jack was left with me. Jack and I always had a good rapport, but that night he was furious. I think probably that was the only time I ever heard Jack—mainly because he was loaded—get really irritated with Neal and start cursing him out. "He was supposed to get her for me, and he's takin' her out to the goddamn car!" Jack yelled. "That's the end of that!" He even started making threats against Neal. "Well come on, you and I'll just settle this!"—that kind of thing. He would get kind of cocky, and he was even willing to challenge Neal—he was gonna tell Neal what he thought of him when Neal came back in. Jack said some pretty hard things—without meaning them at all.

Of course, back in 1946 and '47, I didn't really get to know Jack that well. There used to be a little bar near Columbia—it may have been a restaurant too—where we always used to sit around with some of the guys. It was right by the university, the place where all the fellas went. Everybody used to go in there for hours, sipping on beers.* In *Desolate Angel,* Dennis McNally's got Neal and I meeting Allen there. It tells about us coming to New York and we were sitting in one of the booths when we supposedly bumped into Allen. We did used to go over there quite often, and we may have met Lucien there, since Lucien was always coming in.

Those first few days in New York, Neal and I hung out with Allen, Hal, and Jack, and they were always telling us about things we had to do and movies we had to see. The first one they told us to go see was *The Testament of Dr. Mabuse*—the French version. Like I said, we had thirty-five dollars when we got in to the city; and within two days, seeing films and eating in restaurants, we had nothing. There we were—totally broke in New York City. So Allen very graciously took us over to his cousin's, who let us move in with him. I always know his name until I try to say it, and then I can't think of it anymore. Allen's cousin was a red-headed boy.

In any case, we stayed at Allen's cousin's place for quite a while. Hal and his girl Virginia—they called her "Ginny"—used to come

---

* She probably refers to the West End Bar.

over, and she danced for us up there. She had dark hair, and she was a model—I think Hal finally married her. He always dressed sharp too. Neal was always excited to see Hal. "We've got to go over and see Hal!" Neal would say whenever he heard that Hal was nearby. Hal was an archeology student, and much later I heard that he'd become a farmer in Paso Robles. That's the last thing in the world I would have imagined him becoming! Hal just wasn't the farmer type—at least then he wasn't the farmer type.

When we left Allen's cousin, we finally got a place of our own over on a hundred and thirteenth and Riverside, very close to Columbia. It was right by the river, and it wasn't a bad little apartment—apparently it wasn't the ghetto, but it wasn't the best neighborhood either. I guess mainly college kids lived there. It was a small, two-room apartment, and Jack spent quite a bit of time there with us. Jack and Neal started to get comparatively close then. At that time, Jack always seemed like he never had anything to do—like he never had any place to go, and nothing very pressing. Most of the fellas were rushing here or rushing there; they had this to take care of, and that to take care of. But Jack always seemed like he was at odd ends. Of course, he was out of school by then. He was working on his novel,* but I didn't know a lot about what he was doing. And then, pretty soon, Neal and Allen were getting very involved, and they'd go off together.

It was up to me to support us, so I found a job at a bakery. I had just gotten the job that morning, it was my first day, and Neal told me to steal some money! We didn't have a penny, and Neal told me, like, "Bring some money home!" Well, the woman who ran the bakery caught me, but she didn't call the police. She just dismissed me. It really put me through a traumatic experience—I don't know what

---

* *The Town and the City.*

you would call it, but I went into a state of shock, I guess. Because, after I got off the bus at Columbia, instead of going to the boys' hall, where Neal was waiting for me, I just sat down on one of those big concrete benches that they had near Columbia. I don't remember who it was who found me, but I was just sitting out there in the snow, just sort of sitting there in a daze. In any case, somebody found me, and Neal came out and asked me what happened and what was the matter. The funny thing is, I still didn't feel any disappointment in Neal. It wasn't even so much the horror of being caught. What I told him was that I felt so sorry I disappointed him. I was in tears.

For quite a while after that—or at least, it seemed like quite a while, but maybe it was only a few days, though it felt more like a couple of months—I don't remember exactly—but I would go through these things, these mental episodes, that completely bewildered me. I tried to explain them to Neal. It was as though I was leaving my body. For a sixteen-year-old girl—especially at that time, I had never read anything, never gotten into anything concerning psychology or how the mind works, so I had no way of knowing or even half-ass analyzing what was going on—it was such a frightening, terrifying feeling for me. I was never what you would call a "crier." Before this time, I rarely cried; I wasn't into making scenes or screaming or things like that. But I would get so terrified when this feeling would come over me, like I was dying, and I couldn't stop it. Neal would hold me, literally for hours, walking me and telling me I was going to be okay. It really was a bad, bad time in my life.

Whether this had anything to do with Neal really kind of settling down, I don't know, but it's possible I frightened him. In any case, what happened was that Neal got a job parking cars and we moved over to Bayonne, New Jersey. We weren't seeing hardly anyone—or maybe I should say, *I* wasn't seeing hardly anyone. I guess he would see some of his friends while he was at work, or he would take off

Jack Kerouac, unknown person, and Neal Cassady, auto garage, San Jose, 1952. (Photo by Al Hinkle.)

work or whatever. I'm sure he was seeing his friends. But the fact is, it was still a really bad period for me. And it was especially ironic because I finally had everything that I thought I had wanted. Neal was working and coming home every night, and I was going through this thing of being a good wife.

We had one room with a kitchen, and I went to the dime store and bought paper drapes, and I hemmed them. They weren't totally paper—they were like a paper type of material—and I can still remember sitting there hemming these ridiculous things. After I hemmed them, Neal assured me that they were gorgeous and beautiful. I brought home all these other little goodies. I had that room fixed up, *it was home,* and Neal kept telling me how much he liked it. And then I cooked the first meal for Neal. You know, I'd boiled hot dogs and things, but I was gonna fix him a meal now that we had a kitchen.

I fixed spaghetti for him—God bless his soul! I knew nothing about spaghetti. You know, I never had to cook at home, and so nobody'd bothered to tell me that when you cook spaghetti you have to put it in boiling water. I put it in cold water and brought it to a boil, and I had this sauce that was nothing but tomato sauce. I don't remember if I even had any hamburger in it or not; but, in any case, this spaghetti came out in one big lump! I didn't know what had happened, but I knew it wasn't right, and I was all teary-eyed and upset when Neal got home from work. "Don't worry, honey, it's gonna taste delicious!"—that's what he said, God bless him. I had to slice it and put it on our plates and put this crappy sauce over it, and God love him, he sat there and ate every bite. He really and truly did, telling me it was beautiful, it was terrific, it tasted great. I am a pretty damn good cook now, but I will never forget the first meal in our little kitchen. We laughed about that for years—that spaghetti that I cooked him. We had to cut it off in hunks. It was insane—oh God! But anyway...

Things had finally gotten to where I had everything I'd ever wanted—Neal working, and I had a little home, such as it was. I actually thought it was beautiful. And I swear to this day, I have no idea of why I destroyed it. But when Neal came home from work this one night, without any planning, without it even having entered my head—*nothing!*—when he came in the door that night, it just came out of my mouth. I told him that the police had been there. I swear to you on my grandchildren—if there's more than one—that I tried to analyze it, but I never found the real answer. As the years went by, Neal and I talked about it. Neal had his own theories. He felt that because of all these things that had happened after we got married, that it was my kind of a self-saving reaction—an unconscious thing to get myself out. But I didn't want out. I mean, I didn't *think* I wanted out. Everything was exactly the way I had always dreamed it would be. But then I did that—I went ahead and told him that the police were looking for him.

From the moment I opened my mouth, I wanted to tell him the truth. But of course Neal was excitable enough as it was—that was just his natural state—and when anything happened that would upset him like that, there was no way to stop him from overreacting. There was no way I could've sat down with him and said, "Neal, I didn't mean it, it wasn't true." I couldn't have stopped him even if I had wanted to, because he probably wouldn't have believed me. He would've thought I was trying to calm him down. So I put myself through this total nightmare, going through every bit of this agony with him, and every minute of it hating myself.

He left and ran to get the bus. I had to pack all of our stuff in this trunk and lug it two blocks to the bus and get it on the bus and take it all the way to Jersey City, where Neal was waiting for me. I mean, I was going through these insane things that I was putting myself through—stuff there was no need for. We slept in parked cars. It's just like I said. I've thought about it for years and years and years. If I had sat down and plotted it, or thought about it, it would have been different. But I didn't. It just came out of my mouth without one thought about what it would lead to—what kind of reaction Neal would have.

We went through hell. And then Neal got the bus and went up to Hartford, Connecticut, and he was still thinking about us getting back together. He wrote and told me, "I'm looking for a place for us." Then the next letter I got from him, he said he had found a place for us to live. He wrote, "I've found us a room and I've got a job, and you can come up, in a couple of days." In the meantime, Allen, Ed White, Hal Chase, and the others were very, very nice to me; but I think that—looking back on it—they would probably have been happy to get rid of me. Of course, at that time they didn't know anything about me having lied about the police being after Neal, but I think they would have liked Neal just to be with them. None of them made me feel that way, really, because they all treated me very well. But as I got older, I looked back on it, and I realized that they probably sighed a sigh of relief when I left.

They all chipped in together to buy me a bus ticket back to Denver. When they took me to the bus station that day, they left about fifteen minutes before the bus came in. It went to Chicago or St. Louis or somewhere like that first. But just before it came in, the bus to Hartford came in, and it really was the most awful decision. I wanted to go to Hartford with all my heart—I really and truly did. I loved Neal so much. More than even my love, we had so many things that we had shared together. We were like a couple of kids growing up together. We had shared so many of those dreams and agonies together that it really was a hell of a decision—Denver or Hartford.

PART TWO

*L*u Anne went back to Denver on her own, but Neal had prom-ised to catch up with her in June at the latest, when the college session was over, and they planned to reunite then. Hal Chase and Ed White would return to Denver for summer vacation, and Kerouac and Ginsberg were also planning to come west in the summer, so Neal would no longer have any reason to stay in New York then.

The start of 1947 was a very important season for the develop-ment of the Beat Generation, and Kerouac writes of it in great deal in On the Road. Neal and Allen quickly developed a close friend-ship, and as Kerouac relates in his novel, talked nonstop for weeks on end, staring into each other's eyes and probing the depths of each other's souls. Each had his own ulterior motive—Allen seeking the male lover who had so far eluded him, and Neal wanting to learn to write, or at least to learn to talk the New York writer's lingo so that he could begin to join the club. But to put it in those terms over-simplifies it. Neal and Allen would forge a relationship that lasted the remainder of Neal's short lifetime, and both gave each other an

{ 73 }

enormous amount of validation for the unconventional lives they'd chosen. When they first came together, each had a huge lack of self-confidence—Allen because he was gay, because his mother was crazy, because he'd got into trouble already at Columbia and wasn't living up to the high standard of respectability set by his school-teacher father Louis; and Neal, obviously, because many regarded him as nothing but a "jailkid" and street punk from Denver. The love they had for each other was real, even if it wasn't the particular brand of homoerotic love Ginsberg sought. That love may well have saved both their lives.

Neal and Jack were slower in coming together. Jack knew that Neal was laying down an elaborate con, pretending excessive admiration for Jack's still conventional prose in an attempt to lure Jack into teaching him the literary trade. Jack's mother, Gabrielle, known as Mémère, condemned Neal as what people then referred to as a juvenile delinquent, a petty criminal who'd try to lead her son away from the path of respectability for which she and her husband had groomed him. Jack's parents didn't care what career he ended up in—whether sports star or writer or insurance salesman—but they wanted him to make a good living, get married, have kids, and live a clean-cut middle-class life. Gabrielle sensed correctly that Neal Cassady would be more hindrance than help to Jack on such a path. And Jack, at this period, was still deeply in thrall to his mother's opinions and prejudices. He was starting to break away, starting to test out the world on his own; but her views, and especially her feelings, still carried a lot of weight with him.

Nonetheless, Jack's fascination with Neal was already starting to grow. Clumsy and shy, tongue-tied with women, unable even to drive a car, Jack couldn't help admiring Neal's ability to zoom cars around a New York parking lot and fit them within seconds into a tiny slot, or to pick up a beautiful woman with a look, a gesture, and half a dozen words, or simply to move through the world as if he owned it by right of his kingly body, his impeccable physical grace. Jack respected Allen's intellect enormously, so the fact that Allen treated Neal as a mental equal also forced Jack to give more credence to Neal's intellectual pretensions. By the time Neal left New York for Denver, in March 1947, Jack no longer wanted to go west just to see the mythological West he'd read of, and watched movies about, since childhood—the West of self-reliant cowboys and death-defying gunfighters and rugged woodsmen and indomitable pioneers. He also wanted to go west—maybe now the most important reason for him—to see Neal again, to see Neal in his natural element, to see what Neal was going to do next.

Kerouac's working-class, French-Canadian Catholic world was about to explode. Ginsberg was about to learn that love—gay or straight—was not the simple matter he had thought it. And Cassady was about to go on the ride of his life.

The stage was set for a huge drama to unfold—the drama that would give narrative bones to one of the greatest American novels of the twentieth century. Poor Lu Anne, slaving away at a hamburger joint to save money for her husband's return, had no inkling of all that was coming down the pike at her.

Lu Anne:

Jack came out to Denver in the summer of 1947 to see Neal, but I didn't learn of that until much later. When Jack was in Denver in 1947, I didn't know it. It seems almost inconceivable to me that Jack was in Denver seeing Neal without my knowing about it. I know Jack wrote about it, and Jack's biographers say it happened, and a thousand people have said that he was there, but what was so strange was that Jack never talked about it with me. The big thing when we left New York together in 1949, Neal and Jack and I, was the fact that Jack had never been west before—at least I remember us talking about that all the way from New York to New Orleans. That's why when we took off through the Lincoln Tunnel to New Jersey, Jack and Neal were so excited about the trip.*

Lu Anne in front of car, Denver, circa 1947, during the period when Neal rejoined her after their first trip to New York. (Photo courtesy of Anne Marie Santos.)

But I need to back up a little. A couple of months after I left New York, and left Neal up in Hartford, he came back to Denver to get me on my birthday, the first day of March, 1947. From that moment on, I was completely involved with Neal again, and that's why it's so unbelievable to me that I wouldn't have known if Jack

---

* It may well be that what Jack and Neal were so excited about, and kept talking about, was the fact that their trip that began in New York in January 1949 was the first time they had traveled west *together.*

was anywhere in the vicinity. Naturally I knew that Ginsberg was there, because Allen and Neal and I were all together after Allen came. I know Carolyn says she met Neal in Denver that summer, but I don't remember seeing her there either. If I did meet her then, she couldn't have made much of an impression. I still have a hard time believing he met her there. I may not have the most fantastic memory in the world, but I don't remember either Jack's or Carolyn's name coming up when I was with Neal that summer. Neal didn't even stay in Denver that long, because he'd planned to go to Texas with Allen, and then out to the Coast to join up with Jack.

The evidence of letters indicates that Neal got to Denver later in March, more than a week after Lu Anne's birthday. It's also unclear exactly when Neal met Carolyn Robinson, the Bennington graduate then enrolled at the University of Denver.

Carolyn Cassady, Jack Kerouac and Cathy Cassady, San Francisco, 1952. (Photo by Al Hinkle.)

GERALD NICOSIA & ANNE MARIE SANTOS

What is known is that during the summer of 1947, Neal was doing his best to share himself with three different lovers—Lu Anne, Carolyn, and Allen Ginsberg—while attempting to keep each one from knowing the depth of his involvement with the others. Clearly, from Lu Anne's insistence that she didn't even see Carolyn in Denver (although Neal's pal Al Hinkle says they did meet briefly in a social encounter at Carolyn's hotel room), Neal had compartmentalized his life to an extraordinary degree. Neal also managed to keep Lu Anne away from all the wild adventures, the big parties and swapping of sexual partners, that Kerouac chronicled in On the Road. *Eventually Lu Anne and Allen came to share the same bed with Neal—and while not totally happy with the arrangement, neither seems to have felt excessively threatened by the other. But when Carolyn walked in unexpectedly one day and found Neal in bed with Allen and Lu Anne—with Neal in his usual position, in the middle—the sight horrified her so much that she ran out the door and headed straight for the West Coast.*

A lot of what followed is murky. Different players have left different versions. Carolyn Cassady went to Los Angeles to get a job as a costume designer in the film industry, was told she'd have to wait for an opening, and then went to live in San Francisco in the meantime. Carolyn has written that Neal begged her forgiveness for the sexual contretemps with Allen and Lu Anne in Denver, couldn't wait to join her in San Francisco and resume their love affair, and showed up at her place of work on October 4—after which she took him home to her apartment in the Richmond District and they began living together with plans to marry as soon as he could get his marriage to Lu Anne annulled.

There are a lot of problems with Carolyn's scenario. The biggest one is that the evidence of letters shows that Neal Cassady was in New York City on October 4. After Jack left Denver for San

Francisco in August 1947, Neal drove with Allen Ginsberg down to William Burroughs's farm in New Waverly, Texas. After various misadventures down there with Burroughs and the infamous New York junkie Herbert Huncke, Neal drove Burroughs and Huncke to New York with a load of Burroughs's homegrown pot. They left New Waverly on September 29 and got to New York on October 2. Originally, Neal had planned to stay in New York with the hope that Allen could get him into Columbia; but Allen, feeling that Neal had jilted him, had left from Houston on a ship to Dakar, Africa. Nevertheless, Neal did stay in New York till almost the end of October, and didn't get back to San Francisco until early November 1947.

Although Neal did move in with Carolyn soon after hitting San Francisco, the circumstances seem a good deal different than Carolyn has suggested. Neal's letters to Jack from Texas indicate that it was Carolyn who was pressuring Neal to get back together with her. "She's written me 20 times since I've been here (18 days)," he wrote to Jack. "See what a persistent cat she is." He also told Jack that she was "too middle class" for him. In the same letter, he explained that Carolyn not only "insisted" he spend the winter with her, but offered him the incentive that she would be making a "Hollywood salary" with which to support him.* Considering that Neal had also been having a lot of trouble with the police in Denver that past summer, it is not surprising that he moved on to San Francisco. But as soon as he arrived in San Francisco, he began writing Lu Anne a series of over-the-top love letters begging her to come to the Coast and join him.

All this is not to deny that Neal felt an attraction to Carolyn, though his letters of the period seem to suggest that it was at best

---

* *Neal Cassady Collected Letters: 1944–1967*, edited by Dave Moore (New York: Penguin, 2004), pp. 55–57.

an ambivalent attraction. But versions from Al Hinkle and Lu Anne herself would indicate that he still intended, or at least hoped, to return to his marriage with Lu Anne. After receiving Neal's imploring letters, Lu Anne asked an old boyfriend to drive her and her friend Lois to San Francisco, where she resumed seeing Neal almost immediately. While living with Carolyn, he got a job at a gas station, where Lu Anne would visit him every day; and he told Lu Anne he was saving up money so that he could eventually go back to New York and enroll in college there. The plan, she said, was for her to go with him to New York.

Both Hinkle and Lu Anne relate that Neal was in a state of near panic, and great confusion, when he learned, probably in January 1948, that Carolyn was pregnant. He sought and failed to arrange an abortion for her. "It all happened very quickly," Al said, referring to the annulment Neal obtained in Denver, just before Lu Anne's 18th birthday, and his subsequent marriage to Carolyn. Lu Anne, no longer sure of Neal's intentions, had started dating other men, which pushed him even further over the edge. On his birthday, February 8, 1948, he borrowed Hinkle's revolver, explaining to Al that the only way he could get Lu Anne to sign the annulment papers was to threaten her life. But when he confronted Lu Anne, as she tells it, he demanded she either go back to Denver with him and live with him again as his wife, or else join him in a death pact. When she refused either alternative, he took her out to the beach and raped her, then brought her back to her apartment and ordered her to pack. Lu Anne did not speak of the rape on the taped interview, though she told it to others; and she hints of it in a way on the tape, saying there are events of that day she is leaving out. In any case, she slipped out of the apartment, leaving him there alone with the gun. In an agony of indecision, he tried and failed several times to commit suicide.

At the end of February, he made a nonstop drive to Denver with

Lu Anne, to obtain the annulment before she turned 18. Carolyn's version is that he felt his only chance for peace of mind was to marry and settle down with her. Lu Anne's version is that Carolyn used her pregnancy to force Neal into a marriage he really didn't want.

Lu Anne:

I didn't see Jack again until Neal and I went back to New York in December 1948. In the meantime, Neal went to San Francisco, got involved with Carolyn, got her pregnant, and decided to marry her. But first he had to get his marriage to me annulled.

When Neal drove me back to Denver to get our annulment, it was really the greatest trip we ever took—it truly was. We were all living in San Francisco. Neal was with Carolyn, who was like four months pregnant. We knew we had to do it quick. We only had two days before I was going to turn eighteen, and we couldn't have gotten an annulment after that. So Neal made another one of his nonstop drives.

The judge barely gave us the annulment. Neal was all over me in the courtroom. I'm telling them that he chippied on me all the time, and he'd beat me, and I wanted this annulment. There was a woman judge, and she called us into her chambers. We're sitting there in front of her, and Neal couldn't keep his hands off me. She kept saying, "Are you sure you kids want an annulment? You seem like you get along quite well together." Because Neal wasn't with the program at all; he should've at least acted like he was upset. But when she kept asking us if we really wanted the annulment, Neal started laughing. He says, "No, no, no, I always chippy on her. I'm always running around with other women!" I'm telling her, "He beats me all the time!" and then Neal would give me a big kiss! It was an insane scene. This judge, she just didn't know what was happening, but she finally gave in and we got the annulment.

We were gone for a while—ten days, or maybe a couple of weeks.

We drove back to San Francisco through another snowstorm. It seemed like we were always going through snowstorms. That trip was in March too. When we reached California, we went through the Sierras, and they were still having snow.

Neal Cassady in the driver's seat, on the way to Bolinas, 1962. (Photo by Allen Ginsberg or Charles Plymell; courtesy of Allen Ginsberg Estate.)

PART THREE

Neal married Carolyn Robinson on April 1, 1948, in San Francisco. Through his uncle, Hinkle had already been hired to his life's job on the Southern Pacific Railroad; impressed at his fistful of pay stubs, Neal asked Al to help him get hired too. Soon Neal was earning a good salary on the railroad, and according to his letters, seemed to be enjoying his new domestic life with Carolyn. He hadn't written anyone during those few months of confusion and terror when he had been so torn between Carolyn and Lu Anne, but now he wrote both Jack and Allen about all his newfound pleasures. He also started work on his autobiography, which would never be finished, and which would be published posthumously as The First Third. He especially hoped Jack would consider coming out to San Francisco and getting work on the railroad too, with the idea that they could eventually live and raise families near, maybe even next door, to each other. Although Jack was still working on his first big novel, The Town and the City, he had no money and no real life of his own. He was living with his mother, Mémère, and his sister Caroline and her husband and newborn son in Rocky Mount, North Carolina.

But Neal could not get Lu Anne out of his system. He grew tormented again when she became seriously involved with a seaman named Ray Murphy, and was stunned when she accepted Murphy's marriage proposal. He seemed unable to believe that she would actually go through with the marriage. But Lu Anne, as if to insist further on the finality of their break, went home to Denver to await Murphy's return from a long sea voyage. In a letter to Kerouac in June, Neal made a not-so-veiled reference to Lu Anne as "my cause of neurosis."

On September 7, 1948, Carolyn gave birth to a daughter, Cathleen Joanne Cassady. Neal wrote Jack that she was his fifth child, but only the first one that he would actually keep and raise. Neal seems to have loved the baby a great deal; but in early December, when he and Hinkle were laid off from the railroad, he took the family savings, bought a brand-new maroon Hudson automobile, and asked Hinkle to take a trip with him.

According to Hinkle, Neal never said what the ultimate destination was, though he mentioned "maybe going back to Denver for a while." Although Neal never stated as much, it seems what he was really after was reconnecting with Lu Anne. Because he had been working longer, Al would have unemployment compensation to live on; Neal would leave Carolyn with nothing to live on. Since they needed extra money for the road, Al asked his girlfriend Helen to come along. Helen agreed, so long as Al married her—which he did. In a travel bureau in San Francisco, they also picked up another rider to help with gas money, a sailor bound for Kansas. No one seems to have worried about the fact that, with his limited funds, Neal had chosen to add a radio to the car instead of a heater.

Tired of Neal's smoking pot with Al, as well as his refusals to stop *for food or rest, Helen began complaining quite vociferously. Neal solved that problem by dropping her off in Tucson. Having more scruples than Neal, Al at least gave her his railroad pass, and told her to ride to New Orleans, where she could stay with William Burroughs and his wife, Joan. Al promised they'd pick her up in a week. Then, in the middle of New Mexico, and much to the sailor's chagrin, Neal turned the Hudson due north for Denver. The sailor quickly bailed out, and their new destination—after picking up a certain blonde female who was now wearing an engagement ring—became New York. Of course, there would be a slight detour to North Carolina to pick up Neal's "blood brother," as he had taken to calling Jack.*

Lu Anne:

Neal was driving cross-country with Al Hinkle, and he came and got me in Denver. It wasn't snowing in Denver yet when Neal came after me, so I always thought it was around Thanksgiving, but Al swears it was just before Christmas. In any case, we headed straight for Rocky Mount, North Carolina, to pick up Jack. It took us about six or seven days to get there.

Believe me, that trip across the country was a test of endurance for all of us. It was a grueling thing. I don't remember if Jack wrote much about that or not. Again we had to drive with the windows down because of the frost—and whoever wasn't driving, the other two had to sit pressed against each other. Just to keep warm we had to hug each other. I mean, we practically had to crawl inside each other, because it was cold, *cold,* that winter!* And then, somewhere along the way, we slid off the road and landed in a damn ditch!

---

* Hinkle relates that one of his favorite memories of the trip was when he was driving, with his fingers practically frozen to the steering wheel, and Lu Anne—without seeming in the least coquettish—suggested he slip his hands, one at a time, down the front of her pants to warm them up.

Neal got out, cussing of course. Any inconvenience, anything that disturbed the *plan,* drove him absolutely crazy. He ran off looking for help; and I don't know where in the world he dug him up, but within a very short time here he came with a farmer and these two horses. And they pulled us out of the ditch. We might have set there for two days, because it really was out in the middle of nowhere.

So we went on our way, but it wasn't long before we ran out of money for gas. I mean, we literally didn't have any money. We ended up pawning everything we had except my diamond engagement ring and my watch.* That money ran out too. The only way we could make it across the country was to keep picking up people, hitch-hikers, and getting a couple of bucks from them. Or sometimes we pulled into a gas station, and Neal knew how to run the pump. He'd put in some gas and run it back to zero, put in some more and run it back to zero again, quick before the guy got out and could see what we were doing.

Another time, we picked up an old wino. He wasn't really that old, but he seemed old to us at the time. He was probably in his forties. He told us he could get us some money for gas if Neal drove him home. So, of course, we went like two hundred miles out of our way and brought him home, and it turned out there was no money. That was when I went foraging in his room. It was the filthiest place I've ever been in. It was just a horror. And while Neal was out with this guy trying to find some money, Al and I found these old potatoes underneath the sink. They weren't rotten, but they were old and soft, sprouted, and we found an old greasy frying pan to cook them in. He had a little two-burner stove, so I burnt the pan off to clean it as much as possible, and then I fried those damn potatoes. They

---

* Hinkle tells that he even sold his .38 pistol, which he'd retrieved from Neal—the one Neal had tried to kill himself with—to a gas-station owner for $5 and a tank of gas.

tasted so good! The truth is, they were lousy. I probably couldn't even stand them if somebody served them to me now, but you should have seen the three of us eating them. You would have thought it was a gourmet meal! Oh God, we were so hungry!

We didn't get any money from the wino. That was the first and only time—except for myself—that I ever saw Neal use physical violence on anyone. Neal was not a violent person, and most of the time he didn't get mad enough to use physical violence—*except with me*. And when Neal would hit me, that was simply emotion. I mean, *that's the way it was with us*. It was either loving or fighting, one of the two, with us—especially at that age. But when the wino couldn't come up with any money, Neal was livid. That was the one time he was mad enough to hurt someone, and he hit the guy. I know it shocked Al and I so much, because we knew that under normal circumstances Neal would never think of hitting another person.

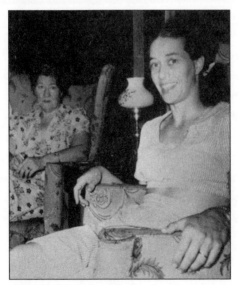

Gabrielle Kerouac and Caroline Kerouac, at home, 1940s. (Courtesy of Paul Blake, Jr.)

What a motley crew we were, my God, by the time we got to Jack's house in North Carolina! Jack's sister had a turkey on the table, which may be another reason I've got Thanksgiving in my head. I had on a pair of Neal's white gas-station coveralls—which he also had on a pair of. We'd been in the car all those days, and I didn't have many clothes to begin with.

Jack wasn't embarrassed at all. He was absolutely fantastic. It was one of the things that impressed me, because I hadn't seen him in so long. Neal had been back to New York on his own, because he had gone down to Texas to be with Allen and William Burroughs, and then he'd driven Burroughs's load of pot to New York.* In any case, Jack's welcome was the most welcome thing in the world—not one bit of embarrassment at all. "Come in! Come in! Come in!" he kept saying. "You're finally here!" And he was so happy, there wasn't a trace of "Gee, Mom, I'm sorry" in his voice. Just welcome, total welcome. Neal was usually kind of oblivious to the impression he might be making, but Al and I both felt a little embarrassed in front of Jack's mother and sister. There we were, so crummy and dirty, and we were hungry too, oh my God! When I think back to it, anything they offered us would have sounded fantastic. And when Jack said, "Come on in and eat!" we were so happy we couldn't believe it, but we were also a little afraid to take him up on it. But Neal immediately headed straight into the kitchen. There was never any embarrassment on his part in things like that, because when someone said, "Come on in and eat," Neal took them at their word. That was one of the good things about Neal. He accepted what people said, until they showed him different. Neal just couldn't move fast enough getting to that food! Al and I sort of trailed hesitantly behind him,

---

* Lu Anne assumed Neal had seen Jack again in New York, but in truth Neal stayed only briefly in New York and left before Jack returned from the West Coast.

looking over his shoulder at the turkey and all the trimmings. Oh my God, were we hungry!

This was the first time I'd met Jack's mother, and I was scared to death of her for what I'd heard. I hadn't met her previous to North Carolina. I had heard that she didn't welcome Jack's friends too readily—and especially people of Neal's type! Neal had told me that she and he had not gotten along too well in the past. It might not even have been anything that she voiced, but just something that Neal felt. But he at least thought he was not too welcome at her house. So naturally, if you're with someone you know isn't welcome, you don't feel too at ease; but she really and truly was very gracious to us. For total strangers to come walking into your home like that, she certainly didn't treat us as unwelcome. Al and I both mentioned later how comfortable she'd made us feel. I was prepared for her to tell us to "get the hell out!"—but that didn't happen at all.

The kindness I sensed was just in the way she acted toward us. I don't remember her talking to us very much. As for his sister, Nin, I only saw her just that one day when we were there; and as I remember, she just sort of reflected his mother, really. I don't remember feeling any particular out-of-the-way welcome from Nin, but I don't really have much of a recollection of her. She always seemed to blend in with his mother in my mind. I understand that Nin died fairly young, even before Jack. I think it must have been hard on Gabrielle when Nin died, especially since it took place in the sixties, when Jack was drinking so heavily. But Neal told me a secret—*he told me that Jack's mom used to drink with him!*

Now at first I had some doubts whether this was true. Neal could sometimes be cruel, and at first I didn't believe him. I told Neal, "You're telling me a story!"—because in my memory she certainly was not the kind of woman who'd sit and hoist a few! But Neal said, "I'm telling you that she gets loaded with Jack!" The thing was that she would rather sit and get loaded with Jack than have him go out to a bar and get drunk with someone else. Having known her the way she was, how close she felt to Jack, I could well understand that. But I still thought it was carrying things a bit far, for her to start drinking heavily at her age. Neal insisted, "It's the truth—she drinks right along with Jack." It's hard for me to imagine her like that—drinking her Southern Comfort, which is ungodly sweet stuff, unless you drink it with soda and lemon. That was the first thing I ever tried to drink, by the way, which is why I remember it so much! When I was about fifteen, I got sick as a dog on it.

When we were in North Carolina, Jack asked us to move some furniture to New York for his mother. It was his sister's furniture; she was moving and giving the furniture to her mom. So Neal, Al, and I agreed to take the furniture to New York, to Jack's mom's apartment, and of course Jack had to come with us, to show us where to put the stuff. That was probably why his mother acted a little more kindly toward us, because Neal was doing her a service at least. On the first trip, we could only take part of the load. Then Jack and Neal turned around and went right back to North Carolina and loaded up the rest of it. I'm pretty sure they put it in a little trailer, because the Hudson certainly couldn't have carried all the furniture. They brought his mother back to New York on that second trip too.

While Jack and Neal made that trip back to North Carolina, Al Hinkle and I went down to the local pawn shop, and this time I pawned my diamond engagement ring and my watch too. Al and I were staying up at his mother's apartment, and I remember leaving the apartment that day and walking it seemed like miles before we found the pawn shop. It wasn't an easy thing for me to do, and I never did get either one of them back. But at least we had a few bucks now to live on, and we wouldn't be broke when his mother got

Al Hinkle with pipe, no date. (Photo courtesy of Al Hinkle.)

back. But I ended up being terribly embarrassed anyway, because the day they got back I had clothes hanging all over his mother's apartment. I was trying to wash all my and Neal's and Al's clothes out, so that at least we would have some clean clothes, and I had them hanging through the kitchen and the bathroom and everywhere! Here we were in someone else's apartment, and it was like we were taking over the place. But again, his mom was really very nice about it. She didn't get mad at all.

During that period, while we stayed with Jack and his mom, Jack was writing a great deal. I always remember him sitting at his typewriter there in the apartment. If I'm not mistaken, he was still working on *The Town and the City* then.* I also remember him working on a story about Neal, but he had turned Neal into the son of a rancher from California. Neal told me about it. He said Jack had given him an Ed Uhl type of history. Jack was using Ed Uhl's life on a Colorado ranch for background about the character based on Neal.**

Of course we couldn't stay at Jack's apartment forever. It was way out in Queens. After we'd been there a while, we went on down into Manhattan and moved into Allen Ginsberg's apartment. When

---

* Kerouac continued to work on the revisions of *The Town and the City* manuscript, which was already under consideration by Harcourt, Brace. The book would finally be accepted by Harcourt on March 29, 1949, but revisions on it would continue until the middle of November 1949. During this entire period, he was also trying to write an early version of *On the Road*. These early drafts of *On the Road* were nothing like the printed version; the characters were all fictional in the traditional sense, with most of their background invented.

** Ed Uhl had grown up on a ranch in Nebraska and met Neal when his family moved to Denver, where he and Neal went to the same high school and frequented Pederson's Pool Hall together. Married shortly after his high school graduation, Ed and his wife, Jeanne, moved to a ranch in Sterling, Colorado. Neal was on parole from Buena Vista at the time; and when he got in some fresh trouble, Ed suggested to the police captain that, rather than sending Neal back to jail, they should just let him work off the rest of his parole time on Ed's ranch in Sterling. Neal only stayed three months, and since it was winter, he didn't do much actual ranching. Nor, by all accounts, was Neal much of a horseman. But Neal would later utilize the experience, especially when picking up girls, by describing himself as a former "cowhand."

Allen Ginsberg, circa 1952. (Photo by John Kingsland.)

we first got there, Allen wasn't working; he was with us a great deal. But then he got a job working nights at a newspaper. All that he had was a living room with a couch and a Japanese table, and then a little tiny bedroom about as big as a bathroom, with just a single cot in it. We were sleeping in shifts, so to speak.

Allen would come home from work at maybe six or seven in the morning, and climb in with Neal and I. God only knows how the three of us managed on that little cot, but Neal was trying to be generous with his attention. So Allen would have his head on one shoulder, and I would have my head on the other. But there was no place for Al Hinkle except the couch; and Al being as tall as he was, he had his problems on that damn couch! But we managed. And by the time Allen got his job, we were getting ready to leave anyway.

I remember cooking spaghetti for us in the dishpan several times. I had to go down the hall to borrow any kind of cleaning implements, brooms and such as that, to keep the apartment clean. But we had some good times that trip. *Jack was there constantly.* You might as well say that he was living with us. He must have gone home once in a while, but he was sleeping here and there, making whatever arrangements he needed to, so that he could spend ninety-nine percent of his time with us.

I got a job working downtown, at the drugstore next to Radio City Music Hall, but it didn't last very long. We had a party one night, and I got loaded. Of course there was always some booze, but that night there was some pot too. There weren't many drugs around—nobody was really into drugs, unless you want to consider pot a drug. Of course they were all doing pot pretty heavily in those days. I remember talking to Lucien Carr that night, and Al Hinkle was there with some little girl that he had been trying to make all that evening at the party. Hal Chase might have been there too. They knew I had to go to work the next morning, so they gave me one of those Benzedrine inhalers to perk me up. I was supposed to be at work at seven o'clock in the morning, and Hal and some of the others took me down. I was in absolutely no condition to go to work. They got me down there, and we went to a restaurant across the street, and they all came to the conclusion that I wasn't quite ready to go to work! So they took me over to John Clellon Holmes's apartment on Lexington Avenue.

Al Hinkle came along with that pretty little girl he was with—she was a blonde, about nineteen or twenty. But anyway, they were going to straighten me up by giving me a bath. The blonde came into the bathroom supposedly to help me, but it came out that she was gay! She admitted to me that she lived with a couple of other girls. When I told Al, he got very upset, and he was so disappointed, because he couldn't believe it! She told him herself after that; but she had been with him the whole night, just talking and partying, and she had never mentioned it. I suppose it's possible she didn't think Al had any romantic intentions toward her. But in those days, I would have called it kind of "leading him on." I can still remember Al's reaction when I told him that I didn't think it was going to work out between the two of them! It blew his mind.

I wound up losing my job, which wasn't really any great loss, because it wasn't too long after that that we left on our big trip west. We were only in New York about a month, but a whole lot of

Alan Harrington, Jack Kerouac, John Clellon Holmes, Old Saybrook, Connecticut, 1962. (Courtesy of John Clellon Holmes.)

things happened during that time. I met a lot of people who really impressed me, and one of the most memorable was John Clellon Holmes.

We actually stayed at Holmes's apartment for a week or so before we moved over to Allen's. John and his wife, Marion, were just great, because they didn't know Neal and I at all, and Jack took us over there and said something like, "Here are my friends, and I don't know what else to do with them—so here they are!" But they were just terrific.

They didn't have an extra bed, but around the living room they had benches with pillows on them. That's where Neal and I slept. Really, I loved their apartment. It was like one big long room, and there was a small room off of that where they slept. John had his table with his typewriter in the big room. Marion went off to work every day, and I remember being extremely impressed with John, because regardless of what was happening in the apartment—and believe me, something was always happening when we were there— he would sit down and write for several hours. Jack came every day, of course, and there were just people coming in and out all the time. It always used to impress me tremendously that John could write with all this chaos going on around him. It just used to blow my mind that he could be so dedicated or self-disciplined, or whatever you want to call it, that he would at least try to write something every day, no matter what was going on.

I was really disappointed and hurt later on when Neal told me that Marion had left John shortly before his first book got published. They had both worked so long and hard together—with her having a full-time job and him writing—that it seemed like a shame that they would split up just before his success. They were both so dedicated—she was dedicated to bringing home the bread, and he was dedicated to becoming a published novelist. It wasn't just talk with

John—he really did his thing! I liked John very, very much. I didn't get to know Marion all that well, because she was gone so much, but they both certainly treated us very nice.

John was very quiet most of the time, and I did notice that Marion was attracted to Jack. It was kind of obvious—even to John it had to be—the way she used to flirt with Jack. Jack, of course, never mentioned it when it was going on. He acted like he didn't notice. I always had it in my mind that nothing really culminated from it—it just seemed like a mutual-admiration-society type of thing. But there might have been a mad, heated thing going on, and I might not have known about it. I do know that Jack never went out of his way to respond to her flirtations. Years later, I heard she had claimed to have had sex with Jack.

But women have a strange way of talking about things like that. On the one hand, when they're being reflective, they'll usually lie their heads off that they never went to bed with a single male except their spouse, or whoever their partner happened to be. On the other hand, someone like Jack, who suddenly became famous, suddenly had fifteen thousand mistresses! After *On the Road* was published, all these women were more than eager to admit to having had extra-marital affairs with Jack, and I used to laugh reading about this one or that one who said they had had a love affair with this or that Beat writer. They would have lied their heads off at any other time if it was someone nobody cared about that they were supposed to be involved with.

I really don't know what went on between Marion and Jack, but I do know that Marion had a crush on him, because, like I said, she was on top of him all the time. And it got to the point where Neal and Jack even discussed it, and I think Jack might have mentioned it in some of his letters, that he was uncomfortable to be around Marion because of his friendship with her husband. He was embarrassed that she was really being so obvious in her admiration for him.

Women were attracted to Jack, and no one could understand why he just seemed to be totally unaware of his physical powers in that regard. It was on that second trip, while we were still at Jack's apartment, I think, that I met his blonde girlfriend Pauline. It was clear that some kind of love affair was already in progress when we got there. She was married to a truck driver, but she was seeing Jack on the side. She and Jack were actually talking about getting married, and he was really involved with this girl, which was rather unusual for Jack. I mean, he was taking the chance of possibly getting shot! Neal was always reminding him that he was gonna get killed when the truck driver found out. Apparently the guy was very violent and beat her a lot—at least that's what she was telling Jack. But she had Jack's complete loyalty, and he was taking chances seeing her, which was not normal behavior for him at all. I remember her quite well. I saw the two of them together quite a bit, and she just didn't seem like Jack's type at all. She was kind of a giggly blonde, and Jack would normally get involved with quiet, serious girls—and usually not blondes. Neal didn't like her, because he thought she was just using Jack to get away from her husband.

It's hard to know how serious Jack was about wanting to marry her. I think Jack, at that particular time anyway, was more involved in wanting to live. He really wanted to just do things—see things, see people, meet people—to become involved in all the life around him. I don't even think he was that worried about his writing at that time—I mean, I didn't get the impression that he felt pressured about getting his book done. Of course, he wanted it done, wanted to see it published and to have it succeed. But I didn't ever get the impression that he felt pressured in any way, or that he was worried whether his novel would be accepted.

Jack and I had a lot of conversations alone, because Neal would get involved with so many people, and of course Allen was always around to distract him. So Jack and I spent a lot of time together, and he talked to me a lot about his life. He was just totally involved with everything that was happening and being with Neal and his other friends. At that period, I think Jack was very, very happy. But in a way it was also like Jack, right then, was waiting for something to happen, like something was gonna happen around the next corner that was gonna change his life. He was going to the New School; his book was being looked at by some major publishers. I think Jack had real good feelings at that time—about everything, really.

It seemed like Jack was always taking us somewhere, or there were so many people coming over to Ginsberg's place, or we would go on little trips to see other fantastic people. The most unusual person we met on that trip to New York was Alan Ansen. One day someone suggested we all take a trip to Alan Ansen's house on Long Island. We all went except for Al Hinkle. That was because Al would sometimes disengage himself completely from us. He always had a way of standing back from the crowd and watching—Jack did that too—but Al would actually go off on his own for a couple or three days at a time, and always came back with a woman! Al was one of those people who was very quiet—you never saw him making passes at anyone or getting out of line or anything. But even as kids, when all the guys would be out looking for women, looking for dates, Al would always sort of disappear and reappear with some girl! Always! Always! He really has, all his life, had a knack for just sort of sneaking up on women. That's how I always picture him, that his quietness was a way of catching people by surprise. He used to always take off—he loves to walk, always has. He used to leave us, saying, "I'm gonna take a little walk—I'll see ya," and he might not come back for a couple days. Then, sooner or later, he'd come lumbering back again, and tell us all his experiences. But he never really got involved with any girls in New York, maybe because he'd just gotten married and his wife was down in New Orleans with Bill Burroughs, waiting for him to come back.

So Al missed this mad trip we made to Alan Ansen's. Alan Ansen lived with his wealthy aunt. I mean, she was very, very wealthy and very society. You can imagine us all arriving at this very elegant house, and it was kind of like Jack described us arriving at his sister's house in North Carolina—only this time we were all cleaned up, and we weren't a motley crew. But to her we *were* a motley crew. She was very society, and she certainly wasn't used to entertaining the type of people that we were. But, of course, Neal was never any different—no matter where he was. He walked right in, said, "How do you do!" and "Lovely house you have here, Ma'am!" and just overwhelmed her completely. Meanwhile, I was overwhelmed by the house. It really was a genuine mansion—it was lovely.

Alan had this fantastic music room upstairs. The walls were entirely covered with his records—just records, records, records, and tapes! And at that time, tapes were a comparatively new thing. In fact, I think wire recorders were still more in vogue. Those early machines used a thin wire to record on. I think they were supposed to be more expensive, and they were the better ones; but then of course the tapes took over, and the wire recorders disappeared. It was upstairs in the music room that things really got kind of crazy.

There is no one in the world like this man. He is unique. Neal was unlike anyone, but Alan Ansen was totally unique in a way that you could never describe. He was gay, of course. He was a huge man—a big, big man—and he was so... Well, in those days they used the expression *nellie*. Unfortunately, he was very unattractive, sadly so, and for a big, big man to also carry himself in such an effeminate way would immediately draw people's attention. He seemed to delight in shocking people. We arrived from New York City by train, and Alan met us at the station. He lived in this beautiful little tiny town, with lots of trees, picturesque streets, and beautiful, beautiful, magnificent homes; and as he walked us back to his aunt's house, he was swishing and screaming at the top of his lungs all the way—just delighting in shocking the hell out of anybody and everybody who was willing to watch. And in those days, the 1940s, it *was* shocking—that's all there is to it.

We had actually gotten to know Alan Ansen in New York City. For a while, he spent quite a bit of time with us in Ginsberg's apartment. Allen used to get disgusted with him because he would come in—a couple of times he did this—he came in and he had picked up a couple of sailors, and everyone was uncomfortable. When you walked into Allen's apartment there wasn't any place to go. You were just kind of stuck there with whoever happened to walk in. Allen Ginsberg got a little disgusted with Alan's antics. He would get a little far-out sometimes and push things a little too far. It was like he was doing things that were totally unnecessary. We were all well aware of what was happening, and it wasn't really necessary to show us all what he was up to—to throw everything in our face. But that was kind of his way—he just liked to shock. At least that's the way it seemed to me. Maybe that wasn't his intention at all—maybe that was his total personality. I have no idea. But when Al Hinkle went to Greece recently, he stopped to see Alan, and he told me he couldn't be with Alan too long. Al told me that he was still the same. "He kind of overwhelms you," Al said, and that's just how I remember Alan Ansen—that you can't take him for too long a period.

When we got to his aunt's house, she was totally unprepared for us, and she didn't make any bones about it. Alan took her in the other room to tell her that we were staying, and she was saying, "Please get those tramps out of this house immediately!" Alan replied, "Go fuck yourself!" I will say, he was equally as open with her as he was with the people on the street. He wasn't having any two ways about it—he told her, "They're staying, and that's it!" Jack and Allen Ginsberg were reassuring Neal and I, you know, "It's all right—he runs the place," and *blah blah blah!* In other words: "Don't worry about it."

So we all went upstairs, and God, we spent hours up there drinking. In fact, I even called San Francisco from his house. I have no idea what his aunt must have thought after that—long-distance phone calls on her phone bill. We all got loaded, and Neal and I got into a horrible fight and had this mad wrestling match in her hall. He knocked me down; but no sooner did I hit the floor than he fell down and started kissing me. It was like something out of the movies. Everyone was loaded; everyone was really drunk, and totally out of line. Alan Ansen put some operatic music on, and he was singing the soprano while I was trying to sing the bass. Anyway, just nonsensical things, but we had a fantastic time. It was quite a night.

Jack and I took a bath together while we were there. I was desperate to take a bath, because there was no place to take a bath at Allen Ginsberg's apartment. I went into Ansen's bathroom, and Neal was gonna take a bath with me, but then he got involved with Ansen or something. I wound up in the bathtub by myself, and then a few minutes later Jack came in. Jack decided he was gonna take a bath too, so we took a bath together. Which was it, we just took a bath—nothing else.

On that second trip to New York, Jack and I were starting to become involved with each other—not as lovers, but as persons. It began at that New Year's Eve party that John Holmes wrote about in *Go*. I was already starting to lose track of Neal—he was always busy doing something. Neal had run off with that girl that Jack liked, and I never found out what happened. Jack and I became dancers that particular night; and ever after that, we would dance together every opportunity we had—as long as we were loaded. You see, Jack didn't dance, and I wasn't the world's greatest; but when we danced together, when we were loaded, I swear to you that we became the most fantastic dancers.

Jack Kerouac "Nijinsky dancing" with unknown woman, Lowell, Massachusetts, 1962. (Photo by William Koumantzelis.)

Jack would throw me up in the air and catch me. I became the most graceful person in the world. Yeah, I was a ballet star, and he was a Nijinsky! We were fantastic together! He loved it, and so did I, because our confidence used to soar when we danced like that. We didn't care who was watching. Jack, as everyone knows, was no extrovert in that respect; and believe me, neither have I ever been. I never want to be the center of attraction anywhere. In a group, a room full of people, I just want to sit back and listen. But in that respect, Jack and I would become extroverts, and happily, when we danced. We just thought we were *so good*. In fact, this dancing bit became like a little secret between the two of us. We really knew how great we were, and we didn't care where we were. When we got loaded, and Jack would ask me to dance, we'd just start doing the Nijinsky moves all over again. We really did it, and it was like the world disappeared. That's something I've never told anybody.

I don't know if there was a secret desire in both of us that we could really dance as well as we thought we were dancing, and I don't know to this day if we were as good as we thought we were when we were together—or if it was all in our heads. People always talked about how awkward Jack was; and when it came to real dancing, traditional dancing, Jack could barely get by. I mean, he'd do a one-two, one-two type of thing—if anything. That's what was so fantastic about his suddenly turning into Nijinsky that night, at the New Year's Eve party. It was as though the world melted away for us, and we just became the only two people there. The really fantastic twists and turns and bending me back—and swirling me around like we were on the huge floor of a ballroom—it was always like that with us, from the first time we danced to the very last. Whenever everybody was busy and we were loaded and there was music on, we just sort of melted into a dance. Whether anybody really paid attention to us—or whether they thought, *Oh, Jack and Lu Anne are dancing again!* and ignored us—I really don't know. But I do know, in our heads, we thought we were Astaire and Rogers! And as we saw it, we really were.

A lot of what happened after that night is a blur to me. The day after the party, Neal found this couple somewhere, and they had some opium. None of us had ever heard of opium—smoking opium—except maybe in the movies. Of course, everyone smoked marijuana, which was a big thing then, especially among the hipsters in New York. But opium, my God! Anyway, he dragged this couple up to the apartment, and we smoked opium with them—Jack, Allen, Neal, and myself. That was the first and only time I ever smoked opium. I really don't remember much about what happened to Neal or the others, or what anyone was doing, after we smoked it.

Jack Kerouac and Hal Chase, Columbia University, circa 1944. (Photo by John Kingsland.)

Part Four

*T*ensions built up quickly in the new year, 1949. Carolyn was
virtually destitute with her new baby in San Francisco, and
since no one else had any money to send her, Jack mailed her $18.
Harcourt, Brace continued to delay in making a decision about
Jack's novel, and he wrote in his journal about having to fight off
vague thoughts of killing himself. Ginsberg, doubtless frustrated that
he now had two major female rivals for Neal's love, grew pompous
and scornful as he warned Neal about "driving his shiny car through
the night for nothing." For his part, Neal grew increasingly uneasy
about the close rapport that was developing between Lu Anne and
Jack. Hinkle recalled that Neal began deliberately pushing Jack
into Lu Anne's arms, knowing that the more he pushed, the more
awkward Jack would feel, and thus the more unlikely it would be
that a real romance would occur between them.

Something had to give somewhere, and the trigger was finally
pulled by William Burroughs, who called from Algiers, Louisiana,
to demand that somebody come and pick up Helen Hinkle, who

had moved in with him while patiently awaiting the return of her husband. She was penniless and a burden to Burroughs, who was also probably uncomfortable to have her witnessing his many forays into the New Orleans underworld as he attempted to satisfy his heroin addiction.

For traveling money, Hinkle sold his leather jacket, and Jack withdrew what was left of his GI benefit checks from the bank. They headed south, to get away from the winter cold in New York, but didn't get far before being pulled over by cops in Virginia— when Hinkle, then driving, passed a stopped school bus—and having most of their trip money taken away under threat of being put in jail. The remainder of the trip became the usual struggle of squeezing gas money out of hitchhikers and Neal pumping his own gas when the attendant was asleep or not looking.

Lu Anne:

When we got down to Algiers, down at Burroughs's place, then I felt a change in Jack. He was doing a lot of talking alone with Bill, and there was a lot of stuff being discussed between them that they didn't share with us. I got the impression when we were there that Bill was very unhappy with Neal. Bill didn't show it in any way, or say anything in particular to us. It was the first time I had ever met him, and we didn't talk a lot with each other, so it was something I felt more than anything he expressed directly. Because, during our stay there, Bill was very kind, very like an old friend. It was obvious he was very glad to see Jack. But I perceived—not a big difference, I can't say that—but something subtle change inside Jack. Jack was still excited about the trip, and clearly happy being on this trip, but I felt something had begun to trouble him. I felt it was connected either with something he and Bill had discussed, or with some impression he'd gotten from Bill—maybe Bill putting Neal in a little bit different light for him. So I don't really know what it was, but there was a definite change that I felt in Jack. He was no longer quite as exuberant over the whole trip.

The coming down to Algiers had been an absolute fantasy for us. We just really had a ball—like the night he described in *On the Road*. We were going through the bayous, and Jack was telling me about Lucien and David Kammerer, and describing in detail how Lucien had stabbed him to death one night in a dark park by the Hudson River. Of course, when we were kids we all used to listen to *The Shadow Knows,** you know, and such as that. We were all nuts about scary shows like that. And we had just been listening to some scary shows on the radio, which is how the subject came up. And then Jack got excited and couldn't keep from telling me his own scary story. It was like he was telling a ghost story to a kid.

Jack was over by the door, Neal was driving, and I was in the middle. I was leaning toward Jack, and Jack had his arm around me, and he was saying in this low, mystery-story voice: "And, after he stabbed him, Lucien looked at the bloody knife..." And he went through the whole thing, one gory detail after the next. I mean, he really did it vividly! He had me sitting there on the edge of my seat, and of course he knew it. And Neal was giggling with him—like a conspirator with him. They were acting like they were gonna do just those very things to me—or like somebody was gonna jump up behind me at any second. That's just exactly how I felt. Trees were overhanging the road, and it was black night all around us. It was really a scary scene, and listening to him and knowing that it was all true made me even more frightened. He was talking in this silly low voice: "And then... And *then!*"—building up to bigger and

---

* The title of the radio series was *The Shadow*.

bigger crescendos. He was doing his best to torture me, but I loved every minute of it.

It was a fantastic trip down to New Orleans; and on that last part of the trip, it was just Neal, Jack, and me. Al had only come part of the way with us out of New York. We had gotten stopped by police when Al was speeding, somewhere in Virginia. Al offered to spend a night in jail, to keep Neal from having to pay the fine, but the cops made Neal pay it. We were lucky we all didn't end up in jail. We were carrying a little pot, but I had stuffed it down my pants, and everything would have been fine, except that when the police questioned us, Neal's story didn't match mine. I was eighteen at the time, but I looked very young, younger than eighteen. It was this small Southern town, and you know how they are, when they sense something that might possibly be "immoral." They decided they would question me by myself, away from the others. They asked me what my name was and what I was doing and where we were going, and I told them automatically I was Neal's wife.

Well, in the meantime, Neal had gotten out of the car because he was furious that they had pulled us over. These kind of things—*anything* like that, that interrupted the trip—used to just make Neal insane! He was outside the car, just screaming and ranting. Well, when they asked him what he was doing, he tells them that he's going back to California to his wife—meaning Carolyn. *To his wife!* Which he thought sounded better, because there were two other men in the car. I could have been with one of them. Well, you know, the stories didn't jibe, and then I had to go through the whole thing of explaining how I'm not his wife now, but I used to be his wife—we just got an annulment a few months ago, and *blah blah blah blah!*

So we all set out together again, but in Florida we needed money, so Al set to work washing dishes. For some reason, Al must have

William Burroughs and Alan Ansen acting out a routine, Tangier, 1957. (Photo by Allen Ginsberg; courtesy of Allen Ginsberg Estate.)

chosen to stay over there for a night. Al joined us a day later at Burroughs's place, where he was supposed to meet up with Helen.

People have talked about how weird Burroughs's household was, with him shooting lizards and Benzedrine inhalers for target practice, and so on, but it didn't seem particularly weird to me. Bill, for the most part, just sat in one spot. I never saw him hardly when he wasn't sitting in his rocking chair with a newspaper in front of him. I mean, I don't care whether if you got up at four in the morning, or it was eight o'clock in the morning or eight o'clock at night, there he sat! He'd sit there hunched over, as if he was absorbed in his newspaper. He presented the image of a quiet, thoughtful sort of person. He didn't seem unusual to me. Because, to be honest with you, by this time I had met a lot of strange people! And when you grow up meeting different sorts of people like I had, you don't really find people that strange anymore—especially as you're growing older. I mean, probably if I had met someone besides Neal when I was fifteen, and my life had gone a whole different way, things like that might have shocked the hell out of me. A lot of the different things that happened to me might have seemed shocking to another person. But, let me tell you, meeting Neal at such a young age was an education in itself!

Neal, of course, has been portrayed as a complete outlaw. And yet at the same time, Neal had really strict rules for himself. For example, with Carolyn, when he got her pregnant, he felt he had to marry her. The same thing happened a year later with Diana Hansen, whom he also married. When he got them pregnant, he felt he couldn't just leave them. No one would ever have believed that Neal had such a moral code—that he would feel that kind of responsibility to a woman—because he gave such an impression of not caring about anything like that. He really and truly cared a great deal about everyone.

The only reason he married Diana, in fact, was because she was pregnant. He was already married to Carolyn, of course. He went down and got the annulment in Mexico from Carolyn. I'm not positive that's what really happened. Neal told me that Carolyn refused to give him a divorce, so he went to Mexico to get an annulment, which he figured was the same thing. There are a lot of different stories about what happened in Mexico. But Diana was getting bigger every day—just like Carolyn was getting bigger a year earlier—and Neal was desperate to do the right thing. Neal told me when Diana got pregnant, just as he had with Carolyn. But this time, Neal wasn't all that het up to get married again. I didn't bother him that much about other women—that's why he could talk to me.

I'm troubled by what Carolyn has written about me in her book.[*] It seemed like in her book—I haven't read it yet—but if the movie script is any indication, it seemed like I was supposed to be following

---

[*] *Heart Beat*, the first version of the longer memoir she later published under the title *Off the Road*. *Heart Beat* was published by Creative Arts, a small Berkeley press run by Don Ellis and Barry Gifford.

Neal, chasing him all over. And it was exactly the other way around. The only reason I came out here to California, for instance, is because of these mad love letters Neal was writing to me: "Come! Come! Come! ... You're my eyes—I'm blind without you! I've lost my eyes!" They were the most insane, mad, romantic letters I've ever seen. And so I came. And then, even after he and Carolyn had gotten married, he showed up at my apartment one day—which Al Hinkle will tell you—and he was gonna commit suicide.* I was either going back to Denver with him, he said, and we were gonna start over and forget all this bullshit, or he was going to end both our lives right there. He was talking like he was tired of it all—this whole domestic life he'd started with Carolyn in San Francisco—and this time he was sure we could make it together, and that was the end of it! He wasn't going to let me turn him down. And he had this gun.

Neal was in pretty bad shape at that time. I don't know what was really happening between him and Carolyn. When we got the annulment, I had accepted that our marriage was over. That was it. I mean, we were still close and everything, but I was now trying to make a new life for myself. But he kept coming over and coming over. But this one morning when he came over—about six in the morning—he was very quiet. Neal was *never* quiet, and this was the quietest I had ever seen him. He just walked in and pulled the gun out of his pocket and laid it on the table, and he told me, "You're either packing and we're going home together, or we're neither one of us going anywhere."

Al Hinkle will tell you how Neal went by himself to ask Al for his gun. We were both surprised by what he did. Like I said, I don't know what was happening really with him and Carolyn at the time.

---

* This was actually about three months *before* Neal and Carolyn were married.

I don't think she'd had the baby yet*—or maybe she'd just had it—but here he had married her, and I'd accepted it, and now he was trying to undo all of that. I won't go through the whole day; but, in any case, he left for a while, but he was supposed to come back and pick me up. When he came back, I was gone. But he made the trip back to Denver alone anyway. Then he apparently had a change of mind and came back again. Neal often changed course like that. I remember how it took Neal a long time to marry Carolyn after we got the annulment. I had been a little miffed at that time, thinking that they had rushed me around—you know, I had to get to Denver before my birthday—and then they screwed around and didn't do anything about themselves afterward. Neal didn't actually marry her till a month later, on April Fool's Day.

Even after they got married, Neal and I tried to make it as a couple several more times. He had me in a little apartment down in Watsonville, where he was working on the railroad. He'd see Carolyn on one end of his railroad job, and see me on the other. I got a job there too. With me living in Watsonville, we were gonna try it again. But it didn't last long because Neal was always so crazy jealous. It was all right for him to live his own life, but he was an insane man where I was concerned. If he even thought that someone was interested in me, he'd go crazy. I got a job as a carhop down there. He would come in on the train and I wouldn't know it, and one time he stood across the street in a telephone booth for eight solid hours watching me, to see who I was gonna talk to. If I went home, somebody drove me home. I didn't know a soul there—not a soul! I didn't have a friend, I didn't have anything. I had a room in a rooming house, and I never talked to anyone, I never went anywhere. He never caught me

---

* Neal's showing up at her apartment with a gun took place on February 8, 1948. Cathleen Joanne Cassady was not born until September 7 of that year.

at anything, but even *that* used to drive him insane! It really did. He used to get absolutely goofy with his jealousies.

After his baby Cathy came, and then two more children,[*] he was kind of torn in his relationship with Carolyn. Having a baby with a woman somehow made the relationship permanent for him. The one thing that bugged the hell out of him was that he had no child with me. He insisted for a long time that my daughter Annie was his. "Even the blue eyes—look at her blue eyes!" he'd point out. There was just no way that he'd accept my having a child with some other guy. I was remarried at the time, to a sailor named Ray Murphy, and had been remarried for two years before I was lucky enough to get pregnant.[**] But Neal came over to the house when I was like nine months pregnant, and I hadn't seen him in almost two years—yet he was livid. "You didn't tell me about the baby!" he accused me, as if I'd been hiding the fact from him. Because I was the only girl Neal was ever with—I mean, women whom he cared about—that he didn't get pregnant. I'm not kidding. He must have had three or four children when we got married that were from girls he'd been involved with. You know, he kept in touch with them; he had locks of his children's hair.

You have to understand, it really was a thing about his manhood. Of course, you already know about him and his power over women, his sexual prowess—what pride he took in it, and so on. I think it really was a blow to his ego that he couldn't get me pregnant, or that he never did. And he wouldn't accept it, because my daughter's father had jet-black hair and black eyes, and the fact that she came out blonde with these great big blue eyes was just further proof, as far

---

[*] Melany Jane "Jami" Cassady and John Allen Cassady.

[**] Anne Marie Murphy was born on December 18, 1950, which was only about a year and a half after Lu Anne married Ray Murphy.

as he was concerned, that she was a Cassady. In fact, he brought Jack over to the house when my daughter was about a year or a year and a half old, and he was showing the baby to Jack, telling Jack, "See? Can you see how beautiful she is? She looks just like me!" And Jack didn't say much of anything. I mean, he knew better. At least he thought he knew better. I mean, we could've seen one another, you know, without Jack having known. But I think Jack felt that he would have known, that Neal would have told him if he'd seen me again. Neal usually told him everything. If there had been a period in there where Neal was seeing me, Jack felt he would have known about it.

Well, I've gotten a little off track from the trip Neal, Jack, and I were making to California. Al stayed on in New Orleans with Helen for a while, and it was just the three of us who set off from Burroughs's place. When I read Jack's account of that trip in *On the Road,* it seemed strange to me, because some of the things he wrote about had actually happened, and some of it he just made up. For instance, he wrote about how we were all driving for a while without our clothes on. That really happened, and it was something else! But when Jack wrote it in the book, he said I smeared—or I rubbed— cold cream all over them, on everything, even their private parts, which wasn't so. Unfortunately, we didn't have any cold cream. I might have if we had had any, but I didn't.

When we were going through Texas, it was so *hot!* Oh, God, it was ungodly hot! And naturally Neal was the first to say, "Let's take our clothes off! At least it'll be cooler." And Jack and I were both a little more shy—a little more reserved. I have never been one that could go nude in front of other people. I mean, I've always been, not embarrassed about my body necessarily, but I never felt that it was the world's greatest either, you know! So I was never very much of an extrovert when it came to sex—and Jack wasn't either, to say the least! Neal was. Neal had a pretty body and was very proud of it. So when Neal first made the suggestion that we take our clothes off, Jack and I kind of looked doubtfully at each other, because we weren't into each other in that respect, even though we had taken baths together and everything. The things we had done in the past didn't seem quite so like throwing your clothes off suddenly. But anyway, with Neal's prodding, we all finally did so.

All three of us were in the front seat. We were just driving across Texas, and we came to these ruins. I always wished that Jack had put this in the book.* At first we thought it was ancient ruins, but I don't really know what it was. There were some great big huge cement blocks and some statues that had been damaged or vandalized. Some of the statues had their arms knocked off, and this and that. But at one time it had obviously been a beautiful thing, maybe an Indian memorial thing of some sort. Anyway, we stopped the car to get out and go examine them, to look them over, and we were all still nude.

Jack and I were extremely nervous; we were, of course, looking for cars both ways. We didn't want anybody to catch us naked. Neal could have cared less. Well, anyway, we see down the road, here comes this car, and Jack and I are yelling at Neal, "Come on! Let's get back in the car! We're gonna go to jail!" But Neal was still examining everything and talking a mile a minute—*blah blah blah!* Finally Jack and I just said, "The hell with you!" and we ran across the highway and jumped back into the car. The car was coming toward us, and as they were approaching they were sort of slowing down. All of a sudden, Neal gets up on this platform and strikes a pose. And the car slows almost to a stop—it was clear the people inside wanted to get a better look at Neal. We could see them. It was an older couple in the car.

---

* Kerouac did include a very condensed version of this scene in *On the Road.*

Jack and I were both in our car, bending as low as possible and trying to keep out of sight. I am not exaggerating—we were both just trying to hide. Neal, meanwhile, is standing just perfectly still. You could see them gaping at him. Jack and I started to talk about it, and we knew exactly what they must be saying. We could see the woman talking to her husband and pointing at Neal, and you could just imagine that she's saying, "Look at these fantastic ruins and *that beautiful statue! It hasn't been marred at all! It's just in perfect condition!*" Because, fortunately, it was far enough away that she couldn't see the difference between skin and stone, and he didn't move a muscle. Carolyn has some pictures that she drew of Neal nude, and some of them are really quite good. They show what a good body he had. I mean, the way he was built, he could have been the model for some of those famous statues. I can still see that old lady sitting there, just jabbering at her husband—just *bupbupbup-bupbupbup!* And he's squinting and shaking his head, as their car creeps away.

Jack and I thought for sure they were gonna stop to get out to examine this perfect, perfect statue—amongst the entire ruins that were around it. I used to wonder if he were going to put that in the book, because we'd laughed over that, over Neal having the guts to stand up there like that. Because when the car first appeared, Neal really couldn't make out who it was. It might have been the highway patrol just as easily. And they would have stopped you for traveling with no clothes on—you better believe it! We might have wound up in one of those small-town Texas cells.

We had some very good times on that trip, but then there were other times when I was scared to death. I thought for sure they were both gonna get killed someplace in Texas. Wherever they stopped, Neal was determined to find some pot. In one town, he got ahold of some Mexican kid, and in those days you used to hear a lot of stories about the Mexicans taking the tourists off and promising them a good deal, then robbing or maybe even killing them. Neal never had any fear of anything like that. He'd go into the darkest alley with the roughest-looking characters. But nothing bad ever happened to him. I don't know if he ever thought about what might happen. Jack was a little more hesitant about following Neal. I mean, he would almost always go, but he would try to talk Neal out of it first—or see if they could arrange something a little safer. Jack would say, "Well, why don't we meet him at a restaurant? Or some place with a little brighter lights?"

What a trip it was! One day we'd be hunting out Mexican drug dealers, and the next we'd be hanging out with wonderful artists. I'll always remember our stopping to see the writer Alan Harrington in Arizona. Jack knew him from New York. He was living with an Indian girl—she might have been his wife—and they were living in this little sort of Indian house. It was not a wickiup exactly, but it was an adobe shack of the type a lot of Indians lived in. These were round adobe houses like the ones the Indians had built a long time ago. I can't think of the proper name of them. But anyway, we stopped, and here he was, the writer Alan Harrington, sitting out there in front of his house, in the hot and dusty desert!

His mother-in-law was in the house cooking beans and frijoles and whatever. He was just sitting there at a little table with his type-writer, and it was *hot,* my God! I don't know what the temperature would have been there in Arizona in February, but it was hot, and he was sitting out there in the middle of nowhere, banging away on the typewriter. There was just his house with a little shed next to it. I think they had a cow and maybe a few other animals—that's what the shed was for. Those were the only things he owned.

It was still early when we arrived, and later in the day he took us over to a wealthy woman's house—a woman who was in her early fifties. She had this big young man—a young kid, you know, with a beard—and she was supporting him while he wrote. Her house was a beautiful, beautiful hacienda. I mean, it was luxury from the word *go*. Neal and this would-be writer and everybody got loaded—very drunk—and the writer made a pass at me. Neal walked in just when he was kissing me. Then Neal and he got into a big argument; and while they were fighting, Jack and I started dancing. Of course, this patron of the arts had a stereo—at that time, not too many people had stereos—and she had all this fancy sound equipment, all built-in and everything. Jack and I ignored the whole jealousy situation— as Neal got angrier and angrier, we just played music and kept on dancing. We spent most of the time at her house Nijinsky-ing.

The guy stood up to Neal, and that's when Neal hit the ceiling. Neal was so mad that he finally made us leave. So off we went, back over to Alan Harrington's house; and we had to say good-bye, because he had no place for us to stay. Jack would have liked to have stayed for a couple of days, but there really was no place for us there.

Anyway, it wasn't too much longer before we got to San Francisco. When Neal had something on his mind, he could be very abrupt and just push everything else aside. He was determined to go back to Carolyn. Of course, he was happy to be home, at that point. That happiness wouldn't last very long, but at that point seeing Carolyn again was all he could think about. He just literally dropped Jack and I on the middle of the sidewalk, and said, "I'll call you guys!" And off he went!

Jack and I just sort of looked at each other. And Jack was hurt—he really and truly was. I was used to it. I knew Neal, and I knew what to expect. I also knew he would be back—with as much enthusiasm as he had left with. But nonetheless, that was something Jack hadn't expected because it was so sudden. I mean, there really were no preliminaries. There was no leading up to the subject—no hints that he was about to depart. He didn't bother to say, "Don't worry, I'll call you tomorrow at ten o'clock," or even just, "I'll see you guys." It really did hurt Jack badly.

We hadn't really made any specific plans of what we were gonna do when we got back to San Francisco; nobody had any real plans. But of course Jack had assumed Neal was gonna spend some time with him. On the one hand, you might say it was kind of arranged by Neal—or something Neal expected—that Jack and I would spend time together. That was expected only on Neal's part. Well, not only on Neal's part—I shouldn't say that. But it was expedient for Neal at that point for Jack and I to get together as a couple. That way he didn't have to worry about either one of us. Of course, Neal had started suggesting this back in New York, started suggesting that we should get involved with each other. That was something Jack

Jack Kerouac, Carolyn Cassady, Al Hinkle, Al's son Mark, and Carolyn's children, Jami and Cathy, San Francisco, 1952. (Photo courtesy of Al Hinkle.)

and I were already feeling on our own, anyway. Neal had talked to us already there, about how nice it would be if Jack and I had a little romance; but the fact is, nobody needed to push it. Jack was already heading in that direction himself; and the thing was, Neal was very much aware of it. And Neal could *never, never* bear something like that to occur unless he was the one who instigated it. You see what I mean?

Neal knew it was happening. He also knew that Jack, being the way he was, and me being the way I was, that it probably wouldn't have come until Neal was ready to go back to Carolyn. And we knew we would have to wait—because once he went back to Carolyn, he could have no recriminations about Jack taking his girl or me not remaining faithful to him. Neal didn't like us setting our own time-table, so he thought that he would start the ball rolling—which, like I said, was totally unnecessary. And neither one of us picked up the ball in New York, as Neal expected, because I think we—Jack and I—did care very much about Neal's feelings, and how all this would look to people. But still, the attraction between Jack and I was growing, and it was something that had nothing to do with Neal. That bothered him badly.

Anyway, by the time we had gotten to San Francisco, it was just sort of expected by everyone that Jack and I were going to be together. *But Jack still expected to be with Neal,* regardless of where Neal ended up living. Neal had Carolyn in their house, and Jack might have me in some apartment across town, but nonetheless Jack expected that the two of them would still be hanging out together. That's why Jack started out on this whole adventure.

In Jack's mind, this whole trip was because of Neal, with Neal, for Neal—whatever. It was a big hurt for him to be abandoned like that. We spent the next couple of weeks sort of consoling one another. The sad thing is that, under different circumstances, I think the outcome might have been entirely different. Things might actually have worked out for Jack and I. But unfortunately we had no money; we had nowhere to go. I talked to a hotel manager at the place where I had lived before, and he let us move into the hotel, on the assumption that we'd be able to start paying the rent soon. It was the Blackstone Hotel on O'Farrell Street. And then I went with a girlfriend of mine over to her house, to get an iron to cook with. She was a singer in the Tenderloin, and I had stayed with her once before. She had taught me how to cook using the heat from a steam iron—which worked pretty well in place of a hot plate. In *On the Road*, Jack wrote about seeing me get in a car with this girlfriend, and he made it seem as if we were working as prostitutes.

Before I had left San Francisco and gone back to Denver—which was several months before Neal came back to Denver and picked me up to make the trip to New York with Al Hinkle—I had started going with a seaman. We had become engaged in San Francisco. When I first moved back to Denver, I still had full intentions of marrying him. But gradually he started slipping from my mind. His ship was gone for a year, and it was due back now in a couple of weeks. But in the meantime, when Neal asked me to go to New York with him, the only reason I agreed was because Neal assured me he was coming back to San Francisco. He promised me he'd get me back in time to meet my fiancé's ship. I said, "Okay, I'll go with you, as long as you realize that I'm not getting involved with you again." I really had a long talk with him, because when he came after me that night and banged on my door, he was still acting like we were married. As soon as I said, "Who is it?" he answers, "Your husband! Open up!" I mean, he still was going through that thing of acting like I belonged to him. But I told him, I said, "I'm going as a person, and not as your wife. I mean, it's not gonna be the way it was. This time, I'm gonna have my own fun in New York." And he said, "Yes"—he claimed he accepted that, which of course he didn't.*

But then in the meantime, before we got back to San Francisco, Jack and I had become involved; and like I said, it had gotten to the point where I didn't really know how I felt anymore concerning my fiancé or the marriage that was supposed to take place. I hadn't seen him in almost a year by that time, and I was even having trouble remembering what he looked like. But I knew that Jack was needing and leaning on me, and *I* needed someone to lean on! But Jack didn't have much comfort left to give. Because especially after Neal left, Jack felt lost. Well, he *was* lost—even more so than I, in a way, because he didn't know anybody in San Francisco. And the way Neal had done it was cold and cruel. So we talked and talked and made plans to find an apartment where we could live together. We even talked about getting married.

The truth is, those two weeks really were kind of a nightmare for both of us—even though we were clinging together like we didn't have anything or anyone else in the world. We were clinging together as the only way to keep going. We just sort of stayed in the room for three days and nights—not knowing what to do, where to go. And Jack, unfortunately, didn't take any initiative. Jack wasn't the kind of guy who'd say, "I'll go get a job," or "I'll go do something!" I mean, he really was more lost—about the whole situation—than I was.

But anyway, after a few days, I went over to see some friends in order to borrow money from them. This is what Jack wrote about in *On the Road*—this was the scene he was apologizing to me about

---

* Al Hinkle claims Neal told her, "You can sleep with anyone on this trip—just not with Hinkle." Al says he later asked her why Neal didn't want her to have an affair with him in particular. He says Lu Anne told him that Neal was jealous of him. When Al asked her, "Why would Neal possibly be jealous of me?" she told him, "He sees you as a success, and he thinks of himself as a failure."

when Neal and I first looked at the book. Jack would always say, "I was mad at you when I wrote this," and *blah blah blah*. What happened was, I went over to see some friends of the fella I had gotten engaged with. I saw them, and they lent me some money—that was all, nothing else. Jack wrote that they were *sailors*; actually, they were *seamen*. And then I ran into another girlfriend of mine, who was going with the fella that owned the bar on Turk Street where my other girlfriend sang. I did get a little upset with Jack about how he wrote that scene. I was gonna go out with her and this guy that owned the bar, hopefully to get a job, because I was still underage. But she was younger than I was, and she was working there. So I figured if she could work there, at least maybe she could help me get some kind of job. That's where Jack wrote: "I stood in a doorway and watched her get into a Cadillac." But he didn't explain about how "she went out and tried to get a job to do something for us"; he didn't say anything about my trying to help him. He was just mad at the whole situation.

Our desperate time together lasted about two weeks. Finally, by that time, Neal called us, and of course he came over like nothing had happened. And Neal took us out to a couple of places—it was just an insane situation. He was acting as though everything was hunky-dory. "It's great, isn't it?" he said. "You kids are over here, and I've got my place on Liberty Street—and we're all just fine!" The truth was that Jack and I were just wallowing in self-pity and misery.

I don't remember now whether Jack talked to Neal, or Neal talked to Jack, about Jack coming over to his house—because by this time I had gotten to the point of knowing that something had to be done soon, one of us had to do something, or we were going to end up out on the street. We could not sit in that room doing nothing any longer, with me trying to borrow money, and our hotel bill was going up. Neal wasn't coming up with anything, any kind of solution. Of course, we only saw him twice. His visits were a boom-boom type of thing. So I told Jack that really the best thing would be for him to talk to Neal and see about arranging to stay at his house, and for me to try to go and stay with this girlfriend of mine—at least until we got situated.

For a while, Jack had been fairly serious about us getting married. We talked a lot about it. He felt it would be the best thing in the world for both of us—the only thing in the world for both of us. But of course, this is the type of talk you have laying in bed in the middle of the night, when you're not thinking about what you're gonna do tomorrow. Jack wasn't thinking about anything except how needy he was at the moment. He was leaning on me. I don't mean "leaning on me" in terms of putting pressure on me. He wasn't trying to make me do anything—nothing like that. I mean, emotionally—he needed my emotional support. And at that moment, I needed someone to lean on as much as he did, and Jack wasn't ready to be leaned on.

In realistic terms, Jack was not actually ready to take on the responsibility of marriage—at least not then—and I knew it. He wasn't ready for any kind of responsibility. And I was confused, because I was thinking about my own obligations. Here I had accepted a ring, and said yes to a man who wanted to marry me. I told him I would wait for him to get back, and I had all intentions of doing so until this wild trip; and then I had gotten all involved back with Neal again. And now, on top of everything, I had really become deeply involved with Jack too. And I can say, had circumstances been different, or if we had had any kind of a thing we could have leaned on—a bundle of money, a place to stay—there might have been a different result in my relationship with Jack. We might actually have gotten married—who knows? God knows I don't.

The only thing I can say for sure is that Jack and I needed something a great deal different than each other at that time. Like I say,

I don't remember whether it was Jack who gave the idea to Neal, or Neal who proposed it to Jack—or maybe I talked to Neal, because we were calling Neal a lot at that point—but Neal came over and picked up Jack. Of course, I still saw both of them after that. I saw them quite often, as a matter of fact.

A little bit later came the famous incident of Neal's broken thumb.* We got back together after I left the Blackstone Hotel. Neal came back to see me, and I decided, "Okay, we'll try it again." I admit, it was an insane thing to do. I don't know what was happening with Neal and Carolyn. Carolyn always seems to think that I came looking for her Neal; "as always" is the way she puts it. Whether Neal told her this or not I have no idea. But the truth is, Neal wouldn't let go. And unfortunately, I didn't let go either—like there was this umbilical cord between us, so to speak. Jack had gone back to New York—this was early 1949. He was so hurt and so disgusted, I think, that he just wanted to get out. He wanted something familiar, the same as I did. We were both in exactly the same position. We were just lost. Somebody just took us and dumped us, and there we were. We were trying to lean on each other, and neither one was giving any support, really. We just weren't able to give anything to each other.

Jack wrote in *On the Road:* "I lost faith in Neal that year." Oh, it was a terrible, terrible period! Because, you know, half of it, like anything else, was just the disappointment when something great ends. You take a trip, and when you get home, there's always a little

---

* During the spring of 1949, after Jack returned to New York, Neal continued to live with Carolyn and his baby, but at the same time he resumed his love affair with Lu Anne, who had decided to go ahead and marry Ray Murphy. Murphy knew about Neal and wanted to kill him, while Neal was furious at Lu Anne for her willingness to "betray" him by marrying anyone else. In the midst of one of their violent arguments, Neal took a swing at her, but his hand struck the wall instead, and he broke his thumb. It was put in a cast and later became infected, perhaps because he had to stay home every day taking care of the baby, and changing diapers, while Carolyn went to work to support the family. The tip of his thumb eventually had to be amputated, which Neal considered his "karma" for having attempted to punch Lu Anne in the face.

letdown. And that, really, could have been accepted. What was so terrible was the way that it was done—the way that Neal just sort of deserted us. And I know Neal well enough to know that he didn't intend to hurt us. I know he didn't even realize that he was hurting us, or what he was doing to us. *Unfortunately, that was one of Neal's worst traits.* He could hurt so damn bad and not even be aware of it. It was unbelievable, sometimes, how he could be so totally unaware that any big emotional thing was even going on. And, of course, a lot of big things were going on inside us at that moment.

There were more than just the feelings between Jack and I, because Neal was mixed up in all of it—for both of us—and we didn't have anywhere to turn except to each other, and we were of no help to each other at all. I've thought a lot about why I even made that trip back to New York with Neal. I certainly didn't go with the expectation of getting married to him again. I went on that trip solely as an adventure. I remember talking to him half the night about it. Because he got to Denver about two o'clock in the morning; and when he came into the room and told me, "Pack your bags, we're goin' to New York!" I immediately said, "Of course." I loved to go anyway; I was always ready. I was like Neal in that respect—it didn't take very much to move me. And I wanted to go immediately, but I wanted him to know I wanted to go on my terms. I wanted to go as my own person, and I was not going to go back into the same trap again. He was not going to be the boss, going here and there, and treating me as his property. I wasn't going to have it that way. Of course, that's the way it turned out.

But the point is, I was insistent. I mean, I was trying very hard to be independent of him. That's why I say a great many things might have been entirely different if we had stayed in New York a little longer. I think it would have made a big difference because it would have given Jack and I a chance to allow our feelings—the feelings that we had for each other—to go ahead and grow, or die a slow death of whatever. We needed time together without all the excitement that was being emanated by Neal, concerning the trip and how everything was gonna be in San Francisco—and this and that. Neal was giving us expectations and feelings and all sorts of things that really weren't there—he was talking about things that weren't real, or they hadn't had a chance to become real yet. And then to get the feeling at the end of it all, which Jack did, from Neal, that Neal just didn't give a damn about him—I really hadn't expected Neal to do that. But at the same time, I knew Neal well enough that I wasn't surprised by it like Jack was. Because for Jack it really was a shattering blow.

I can still remember when we climbed out of the car, and Jack was standing there on the curb looking after the Hudson as Neal pulled away. It was as if Jack were thinking, asking him, *What happened? Why is he doing this to me?* And, in truth, it had nothing to do with Neal's feelings for me or for Jack, or with our feelings for him. But it came as a total letdown, especially since Jack had given everything, all the money he had. When Neal dropped us off, we didn't have anything. What little money Jack had had, he had given for the trip—and yet there wasn't a backward glance on Neal's part. He didn't ask, "You guys gonna be all right?" or anything about how we were gonna manage.

From the moment we got into San Francisco, Neal was looking for some place where he could drop us off. As we're driving along, Neal says, "Well, where do you want to go?" And I looked at Jack, and Jack looked at me, and there was no place for us to go! The only thing I could think of was the hotel I had stayed in when I was here before, and so I said, "I guess, O'Farrell Street." That was just what Neal wanted to hear. "Fine, fine," he says. "Oh, that's great, that Blackstone Hotel! Fantastic!" And then when we got there, Jack asked me, "Have you got any money?" and I says, "No, I haven't got any money." You know, we hadn't had any money for days! And he said, "What are we gonna do?" And I said, "Well, I don't know whether I can or not, but once before the manager of this hotel had let me stay, and then I paid him later." So I told Jack, "All I can do is try. Keep your fingers crossed, and I'll go find out." So I went in and talked to the manager, and luckily at least we got a place to sleep.

We got the room, and then I took him immediately over to that girl's house to see about getting us some food, because we hadn't eaten anything either. Neal was going home—he knew Carolyn would have some food. So I got us some food, and after that we were just sort of floating. Like I said, we would just stay in the room three and four days at a time, not knowing what else to do or where to go or anything. I mean, had I been a little older I think I might have handled the situation better, but I was in a rather confused state by that time myself. I knew that I had created a lot of these problems because I had allowed myself to get involved with Neal again.

My feelings for Jack were deep, and they were honest. But Jack and I didn't have anything to build on; we didn't have anything to hang on to. We didn't have anything, period—let's put it that way. And even though we could lay there at night and talk about being together forever, and talk about marriage, we both really knew, I guess, that we were just talking. Because how were we going to start a life together, unless Jack had taken the initiative and said, "Well, I'll wire home and get some money, and we'll both go back to New York"? But it was as though he was worse off than I was. He really was; he was the most lost person I had ever seen. Since I first met him, he'd always seemed at odd ends, like he had nothing to do in the world—nothing except write, of course—but now he just seemed at a total loss about everything.

It's the first time I have ever mentioned this to anybody, but the first night after Neal left, *Jack laid in my arms and cried like a baby.* He really did. He was really, really desolated and hurt. We had some pretty long, deep talks. We thought we had everything sorted out. Of course, then morning would come and we'd be faced with another day of "Where are we gonna eat?" and was the manager gonna throw us out? And it didn't seem like Jack had any plan at all. It was like he was kind of waiting for me to do something. At times like this, he could be completely passive, and just let other people decide what was gonna happen. But especially right then, I needed someone to say, "Okay, now, let's take some action." I would have worked with him and done whatever there was to do. But I also needed someone to encourage me, and give me confidence that we could get out of this mess. But like I said, Jack was in really worse shape than I was.

Coming back to San Francisco had turned Jack's whole world upside down. He wondered why he had made the trip, even—what had gotten into him, what had made him so excited to make this mad trip out to the Coast. Here he was, penniless and friendless—or so he felt—and for what? He was questioning every single thing in his life. It was like I wasn't even there, like I wasn't the same girl that I was before, the girl he'd been so attracted to, the "beautiful little sharp chick" with all the "golden ringlets" that drove all those Columbia guys crazy. I had lost some of my appeal for Jack, just like San Francisco had, when the supercharger was no longer behind us.

Neal had been pushing me into Jack's arms. For a couple of weeks, while we were getting ready to leave New York, Neal was becoming aware that Jack and I were spending more time together, that we had feelings for one another. And Neal never allowed something like that unless he dictated it or sort of arranged it, you might say. His ego wouldn't let something like that happen. It was especially troubling for him because he had brought me to New York, and now he was seeing that—if he left the situation alone—things might go their natural way and I might decide to stay in New York with Jack. Neal would never have gotten over that. He started, not literally telling Jack what to do with me, but letting Jack know what he was thinking. He'd encourage Jack by telling him, "Why don't you and Lu Anne talk together?" Or he'd just set up situations where Jack and I would be by ourselves.

There was no way Jack would have ever made a pass at me as long as he thought Neal was in the picture. I mean, he wouldn't have. He wouldn't have come near me. Even though we were both well aware how we were feeling, if he thought for one second that I was still Neal's girl, that Neal was there as my lover, Jack would never have shown the least interest in me. He would have kept away from me—out of fear of Neal. Not fear physically—I don't mean that. I mean, Jack would have been afraid to overstep, to compete with Neal. I'm absolutely sure of that—Jack wouldn't have allowed a competition thing to arise. Jack would never have gotten romantically involved with me unless Neal was either giving his blessings, or else completely out of the picture.

What happened, finally, was that Jack and I, on our own, sat down and had a talk in New York. We made our own agreement that when we got to San Francisco it would be us, and we would go our own way and find out what was happening between us. That was where I told him that there was the possibility we might end up together. But as long as we were in New York and Neal was there, Jack and I agreed to keep our feelings quiet. Neal knew nothing about this till later.

Jack and I never had any kind of sexual relationship in New York. Oh, he had kissed me, you know! But he never even tried to do anything more. *Never!* Of course, we held hands constantly; we were constantly touching each other. *And dancing!* And really, really enjoying one another—I mean really enjoying each other's company. That's what I said, how I explained it to Neal, when Neal suddenly woke up and became aware of this budding romance. It was because he was so busy doing his own thing, having his own fun, that it slipped by him—and he was *furious* when he realized that here was this thing flowering under his nose and he'd missed it! It killed him that he hadn't realized what was going on. Just like that, Neal could become something else—I mean, he became very, very possessive, at least with me. Anytime he walked into my house, it was like the years hadn't gone by. I still belonged to him—that was the end of it. There were no questions or anything I could say that would change that. After Jack had gone over to stay at Neal's, they still came over regularly to see me; and when Jack and I talked after that, we both just accepted that Neal and I were still together.

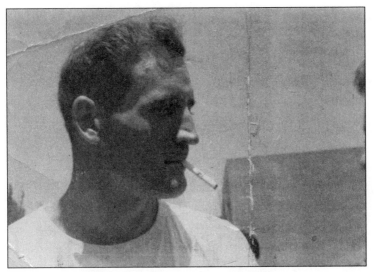

Neal Cassady, no date. (Photo courtesy of Anne Marie Santos.)

Part Five

*1*949 *was a year when great changes were beginning in America—the Cold War was deepening; the Korean War was just a year off; racial unrest was escalating rapidly toward the explosive, if nonviolent, birth of the civil rights movement only a few years later—and great changes were about to overtake the lives of Neal, Jack, and Lu Anne as well. Jack would become a published author, first with a book,* The Town and the City, *that sold only a few hundred copies, and then with a second book that became a controversial national best seller,* On the Road. *Neal too would become a national celebrity, but as the criminal hero of Jack's best seller, and the notoriety would help land him in San Quentin for two years. And Lu Anne would marry, have a baby, divorce, and go on to marry two more times—while never finding any other man she could love as fully and deeply as she did Neal Cassady.*

Lu Anne:

   It didn't take much time before Neal and I were heavily involved again—even though my fiancé hadn't yet arrived back in town. Jack decided to return to New York, but in the meantime Jack and Neal would sometimes take me out together. Jack wrote in *On the Road* about the three of us going to hear a saxophone player at an all-black dance over in Oakland. The dance was in an all-black neighborhood, which none of us even thought about—just didn't—because in Denver there were no neighborhoods a white person couldn't go into. We weren't that racially aware, I guess, because it came as kind of a shock when we went over there with this black saxophone player, who was a friend of Neal's, and suddenly found ourselves in a hostile situation. The place wasn't too full at the time; and when we walked in, Neal immediately went up to the bandstand with his friend. Jack and I walked over to a table, and I started to sit down. I was all dressed up in heels and a suit. Just as I'm taking my seat, this black guy in back of us pulled the chair out, and I went *ploooof!* I landed right on the floor. Jack didn't know what to do. He jumped up immediately to help me up, and he was looking wildly around. We both suddenly became aware of the tension, which you could have cut with a knife. The hate in people's eyes was fierce. It was like they were thinking, *What are these intruders doing in our place?*

None of us had experienced anything like that. It had never even entered our heads that the black people might not want us there. Neal was totally unaware of what was going on. I told Jack, "Just forget it. Let's sit down, and don't say anything." But then I had to go to the restroom. We sat there, and Jack was getting more and more nervous. We were waiting for Neal to come back to the table to tell him, "Let's get the hell out of here!" But Neal wasn't coming back, so I finally got up and went into the restroom. Three black girls cornered me in there. I had to tell them I was a whore. Now, I knew absolutely nothing about whoredom! Not even the tiniest little hint of how they're supposed to act. But that was the only way

I could get out of that restroom without getting beaten up. They're asking me, "You working this territory tonight?" I said, "Well, you know, I just thought I'd drop in." I can still remember telling Jack about this stupid conversation. "I'm just droppin' by." I don't know what I'm saying, even. All I know is that they're not letting me out of that bathroom. They were *hot!*

When we finally got ahold of Neal and told him, "Let's get the hell out of here!"—and tried to explain to him that things were not right—Neal called us crazy. He said, "You're both nuts! Don't be ridiculous!" When we walked out of there, it was like a mob scene in a movie. I wish Jack were here to tell you, because *he was as scared as I was.* You know how in those mob scenes, when someone's trying to walk through, they have to just keep shoving to get a little space in front of them? Believe me when I tell you, when we were walking out of that place, that's exactly how we went through that crowd. Thank God, this friend of Neal's was off—he was taking a break—so he went first, and then Neal, and then me, and Jack in back of me. That crowd did not want to move to let us go through. You know, there would have been plenty of room, but the people had all moved in close around us, to block our way. Jack said he thought any minute he was gonna get a knife in the ribs.

Neal would go anywhere without even thinking. But until then, none of us had ever worried about racial problems either. We'd never encountered any kind of racial anger before. In Denver, we used to go to the Rossonian, over in Five Points, which was a black area, but we never encountered that kind of hostility. And let me tell you, it was a bum experience. It scared the hell out of Jack and I. I don't think Neal really believed us even after we told him all the things that had happened while he was standing at the stage. Of course, he was loaded to begin with. But they had made it very, very clear that they didn't want any part of us in their club. We were intruders there.

In that short period before Jack took the bus back to New York, I saw them both quite often. They would come and pick me up, and we'd go wherever. I didn't get too much of a chance to talk to Jack. When he told me he was going back to New York, we both had a few tears and talked about our old plans to live together in New York. And he talked again about his coming back out here someday when we would both have our lives settled. He would have things straightened out, and I would have things straightened out. And in the meantime, the fella that I was supposedly engaged to would be back, and I would either do what I had promised—marry him—or else rid myself of the obligation—one or the other.

Lu Anne did marry Ray Murphy later in 1949, but it solved nothing for her.

Lu Anne, her second husband, Ray Murphy, and baby Annie, Stanyan Street, San Francisco, circa 1951. (Photo courtesy of Anne Marie Santos.)

Neal's obsession with her, his need for sexual connection with her, never stopped. And Murphy proved an exceptionally jealous, violent, and physically abusive husband, especially when he was drunk, which was often.

Lu Anne:

After Jack left on that bus for New York, I didn't see him again for about two and a half years. The next time I saw him was in 1952, when he was living with Neal and Carolyn on Russell Street, on Russian Hill.

Not long after Jack went back to New York, Neal and I decided to get back together again, to actually live together as a couple, and we moved into a hotel downtown. We got into this terrible fight, and he took a swing at me, but he hit the wall instead of me! Later, he would always say that was his own retribution for taking a swing at me. But anyway, he hurt his thumb pretty badly. I don't remember if I ran out of the hotel room, or if he left; but in any case, one of us left the room. Neal ran to his mother, as usual. Jack had a real mother to go to; Neal had Carolyn. After Carolyn took him to the hospital, he called *me* from the hospital—Carolyn not knowing this, of course. Then I rushed out to the hospital, and Carolyn was there in the waiting room. As soon as I saw Carolyn, I turned around and left. I don't know if she realized Neal had just called to let me know where he was; otherwise, I would have had no way of knowing what happened. I had no idea he had broken his finger. I had no idea that anything had happened.

Neal had to wear a cast for months. His thumb got infected, and he lost part of it. The whole thing went on for about a year. He hurt it again after he hurt it the first time. Neal always said, "I had no business taking a swing at you anyway." He felt that was why the thing was causing him so much trouble. He ended up hurting it some other way—something else happened to it—and the next thing I know, he had all these wires on it, and it was encased in plaster and everything else. He really had a bad time with that thumb.

Jack came to see him that summer, I think. That was when Carolyn threw them both out, and he and Jack drove back to New York together. Neal got involved with Diana Hansen there, got her pregnant and married her, and then divorced her in Mexico, or so he claimed. Anyway, by 1952 he was back in San Francisco, living with Carolyn and working on the railroad. They had two more children by then, Jami and John.

The next time I saw Jack was when Neal brought him over to see my baby, Annie Ree, who was a just a little over a year old. And then I saw him, met him, one afternoon—I don't know if Neal ever knew about it, if Jack ever told him about it. It took place one afternoon, right around the corner from my house, when I lived on College Avenue and Mission Street. It was just kind of a sweet time—we spent about four hours together. We met in a café, and we finally went back over to the house and talked for a while more, because I had the baby, and she was still small then. He was telling me that he thought he had things pretty well together. He wanted to know if I was happy, and if things were going right for me. Things weren't going right, but I didn't tell him anything about that. I told him that everything was fine and that I was happy with the baby. And he told me that he was getting along.

But he was troubled about his relationship with Neal and Carolyn. He said he wasn't going to stay with them much longer. He was planning on going down to Mexico to live near Burroughs. He just said he couldn't continue staying with Neal and Carolyn, but he didn't go into a lot of detail. I don't know really how long he did stay with Neal and Carolyn after that. He told me that he and Carolyn had become involved—that Neal had kind of gone through the same scene as with Jack and I, that Neal had pushed them together. And then that it had gotten to be a tempest-in-a-teapot kind of situation. That's all he said about it. He said there were things that he had been thinking about wanting to do, and that he thought he was just ready to leave. This could have been around spring 1952, because I left San Francisco myself not too long after that, and Jack was already gone. After that day at my house, I only saw him twice more with Neal. And then I didn't see him again until he moved to Berkeley in 1957.

I saw Jack three times when he was out here in 1957. Al Hinkle and Neal and I went over to see him when he was staying in that little cottage over in Berkeley with his mother. It just happened to be the day his box of *On the Road* books arrived—none of us knew he was going to get his book that day. And of course we were all totally thrilled—*Jack's first book!**—and I can still remember Jack sitting at that big old round table with the stack of books in front of him. All of us were bending over him—hovering over him—and flipping through the pages and trying to read this and read that. And Jack was going through agony—he really and truly was. He kept apologizing to us. He says, "You gotta understand now, I was mad at you here... I was mad at you here...." He was apologizing to us through the whole book, and you know we could've cared less. We were just so excited that Jack had had a book published, and I don't think any of us—at least *I* didn't—we never really thought about Jack being famous. It wasn't about fame—that wasn't *it*. What made us so happy there that day was just the togetherness and the fact that he had done it. There it was, and it was in print! But he was just completely embarrassed. I guess all of these things kept flooding

---

* Lu Anne either didn't know of, or had forgotten, the publication of *The Town and the City* in 1950.

down on him. He would remember this line that he had written maybe about me, or some story about Neal, something bad Neal had done—but none of us would have taken offense. I might have called him on a couple of things; in fact, later, I found lots of little things in *On the Road* that just didn't match what I remembered.

But the discrepancies, or the things he had changed, were all he could think of—that's where his head was. He said, "Now you gotta remember, I was mad at you here—that's why I wrote that." On another page he smiled sheepishly and said, "I know this part is just a little bit off, but I had to write it that way." And yet he was also excited and happy over the strange coincidence that all of us wound up together on the day that he got his book. And he was eager to celebrate with us. In fact, after we had closed the book, after we'd kind of gotten our fill of going through and looking for parts about ourselves, we went over to this friend of Jack's, just to get out of the house and away from his mother. Then Jack relaxed, started becoming himself and enjoying all of us being together again. But up until then it really was a painful experience for him. I really felt sorry for him because he was feeling so ashamed. Actually, I think Al and I talked about it later. The way he'd reacted made us more eager really to read the book simply to find out why he was acting like that—why he was in such a state. Al and I had the feeling that there must really be something bad about us in there.

Because when you're going through a book like that, just reading a line here and there, you're not getting any real sense of it. Without meaning to, Jack had made us all a little more curious than we might have been otherwise. Of course, we would all have read the book in any case. Even if it had been the greatest flop in the world, we would have thought it was great, because it was our friend who had written it. But Jack was sure Neal would disapprove of it; he was in total agony from the minute Neal laid eyes on it. I mean, it was obvious he really didn't want to show us the book—he didn't want any of us getting into the book. And if we were going to read it, he didn't want to be around when we did. He couldn't stop making excuses and apologies for different parts that he knew weren't quite right. He'd say, "You've got to understand that I had to change a few things here and there." But none of us really cared.

Afterward, Neal and I discussed the book many times. Well, in the beginning, Neal was thrilled. I mean, no one could have given Neal a finer compliment—in his eyes. He was proud that someone found him interesting enough to be written about, but especially someone that he thought so much of as Jack—someone he admired as much as he did Jack. The strange thing about the two of them, when they were with each other, it seemed like they were totally unaware of the other one's real feelings. This was true even for Neal—even though he knew Jack had written so much about him. I mean, they knew that they cared for each other; but I think on both of their parts they felt the friendship was unequal. They, Jack and Neal, each felt it was more on their part than it was on the other side. Do you understand what I'm saying?

They were both very envious of one another. It never interfered with their association, but it was a very obvious thing when you'd see them together. Everything that Neal was, Jack would want—had wanted—would like to be. And everything that Jack was, Neal would have given his right arm to be, or to have. Neal not only envied the schooling Jack had; he also envied the football thing, the athletic ability, the good looks, the ability to sit down and write the way Jack did. There were just so many things Neal didn't have that had come naturally to Jack. And on the other hand, on Jack's part, he envied Neal for his powers with women, of course; but he also envied Neal's whole attitude, the confidence that Neal projected that Jack lacked. Neal's ability to go anywhere and to act sure of himself was something Jack was very envious of Neal about. I think the women part of it was a small part. I mean, Jack was very envious of Neal's ability to talk to women so easily, and talk them into anything so easily, but I think that's on any man's mind.

The tragedy was that they never seemed to be aware of how great, how deep, were the feelings each one had for the other. Maybe in later years they started to understand a little. But I know in the beginning years they didn't. Neal was always apologizing to Jack. Like when Neal would write letters to him, it was a constant series of apologies. "I'm sorry, well you know how I can't write," Neal would always begin. "I can't write letters—I'm lousy at letter writing," and *blah blah blah.* It was torture for him to write to Jack because he felt so inadequate because of Jack's writing. Neal even felt that his handwriting was bad, and he didn't feel that he expressed himself well.

Neal Cassady and Natalie Jackson, San Francisco, 1954 or 1955. (Photo courtesy of Anne Marie Santos.)

On the one hand, I think when Jack made Neal the hero of *On the Road*, it changed Neal's whole life. He was extremely proud, but I think it also started a thing with Neal that he felt he had to live up to. *On the Road* put Neal on a road of what I would call self-denial. I don't know if that word is applicable or not, but that's what it seemed to me. Neal would deny himself certain things— things that he would have done, or would like to have done and might have done—simply because of this image of him that was growing in people's minds and that he felt he had to keep up with, the image of Dean Moriarty from the book. There was this image now that people had of him—in a way, it meant he had to start performing for Jack, and for other people too. I don't mean it was necessarily just about how Neal related to Jack. I think Neal felt he had to perform, period—especially as the years went by. Because, when Neal was young, he did have a great deal of ambition, and somehow that just disappeared.

I know that we all look at Neal in different ways, but I was maybe the only person that Neal stayed close to through all the years; Neal stayed in touch with me always. He came to me almost any time there was some kind of a trauma in his life—like when Natalie Jackson committed suicide.* That happened in the fall of 1955, when Jack was out here for that big poetry reading. I didn't see him then, but I stayed with Neal for two weeks after Natalie's death. I really, really was worried about him. I thought, if Neal ever came close to suicide, that was it, because he felt he had let her down. I think that was a big turning point in Neal's life too,

---

* Natalie Jackson was a lover with whom Neal had set up housekeeping in San Francisco. He talked her into forging his wife Carolyn's signature on a bank document, so that he could withdraw $10,000 to implement his latest betting scheme at the racetrack. Neal lost the money; and Natalie, filled with guilt and afraid that she was about to be arrested, jumped to her death from the roof of her apartment building.

because every girl he ever brought to me after that seemed to be a girl that he felt needed him, a girl that had some kind of problems. Not necessarily problems with paying the rent or that kind of thing, but psychological problems. After Natalie's death, it seemed like the girls he was being drawn to were the ones that really leaned on him—because he felt he'd really let Natalie down so badly, and he was somehow trying to make it up by helping other girls who were troubled in a similar way.

It was a very bad period for him after Natalie died. When he called me, for the first two days all we did was sit together in their apartment, and he just wanted to tell me about her. I just let him talk. He had little notes that she had written him and left for him. I guess she went out to the roof when he was sleeping or loaded or whatever. And he would read these notes over and over and over, trying to find something in them that would take him off the hook— do you know what I mean? Anything that would show he wasn't to blame for her death.

I've heard people say that the things Jack wrote about Neal in *On the Road* were the things Neal was least proud of. If that's true, the book would only have added to all this guilt he was already carrying around.

Part Six

——⟫•⟪——

There's no doubt that Lu Anne played a significant role in the Beat Generation, but in one respect her viewpoint was unparalleled, in that she was the only person who observed the tandem procession of Cassady and Kerouac to their nearly identical, self-induced deaths.

Lu Anne:

The funny thing is that Jack was going down, in his own way, at the same time that Neal was. When I saw Jack in 1957, I was shocked by how changed he was. The only occasion when I was over at his little house, where he lived with his mother, was that one day when I showed up with Neal and Al Hinkle. But I also saw Jack a couple of times after that over in San Francisco. Neal was not with me on those other two occasions. I met him down on Broadway one afternoon—I parked about half a block from Vesuvio's—and we only spent about three or four hours together. That was when I first became aware that Jack was drinking. Before that, I had never seen Jack drunk—never. I mean, I'd seen him feeling good a little, you know, when we were all drinking. But Neal was never a drinker. Neal never drank anything but beer. Back in those early years, none of us were real drinkers. We could all get drunk on two or three drinks. No, I had never seen Jack drink before. That's why I was concerned and surprised to see him drinking steadily, just one after another.

I was also surprised because Jack was, at that time, kind of putting pot down. He was not really ranting or anything; but unlike the old Jack, he had become very critical of other people. Before, Jack would not have expounded on much of anything, to any extent like that. In fact, Jack used to get loaded on pot all the time! He was always smoking pot with Neal. Pot was just sort of a standard in their group. It was no big thing or anything anybody even thought about. I saw Jack high plenty of times, but I never saw him drunk—I mean, the way he started getting drunk that day. I never got the sort of impressions that I was getting now about his drinking—that it was making him mean and argumentative. I mean, he was *drinking!* He was drinking hard liquor that afternoon. Both times I saw him in San Francisco he was drinking hard liquor—I think it was whisky. I know he wasn't drinking beer, which is what he usually had drunk before. He and Neal would always just have a few beers together.

We had hard liquor when we had parties and stuff like that, but we'd have a few drinks and that would be all. Jack wasn't that interested in hard liquor back then. Except that one time in 1948, when he was having so much trouble with that blonde girl Pauline, the one who wanted to use him to get out of a bum situation with her husband. It seemed like every time Jack saw her, she always had some kind of problem that Jack was gonna have to attack. She kept egging him on, telling him about her husband beating her up. Jack was feeling a lot of pressure because it wasn't a situation he was prepared to take over. He wasn't prepared to take on some truck

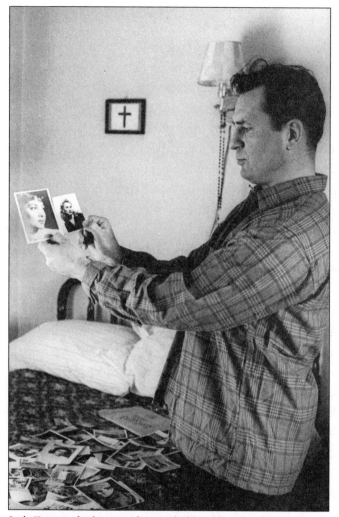

Jack Kerouac looking at photos of old girlfriends in his bedroom, Northport, Long Island, 1964. (Photo by Jerry Bauer.)

driver, you know, and rescue the fair maiden, and she wasn't the fair maiden to begin with. Neal was really upset about it. He told me that Jack had started drinking with her, that she was a drinker and liked the hard stuff herself.

The second occasion I met Jack in San Francisco, in 1957, we had a better time together. I met him up on Grant Avenue, and we left there and went out to Golden Gate Park, where we spent the whole afternoon. When we first met and we started talking, he was the same old, soft, loving Jack. And then, as the afternoon wore on, he started making more and more trips across the street to this bar—I still know exactly where it is. It was called the "Park" something. I went over with him a couple of times. We sat down and had a couple of drinks together. But it surprised me how he began to change after he'd been drinking for a couple of hours. How could I describe it? He became totally unlike himself, totally unlike the Jack that I had known. He was opinionated about things, and Jack had never been that way. I mean, of course Jack had had opinions, but not like now. Now he was expounding on certain things; and as he drank, he just seemed like he grew harder, like he wasn't gonna let any feelings come through. Or like he wanted to forget the feelings he had. I can't quite explain it. It was like he didn't want to let himself show any of the old tenderness he used to feel for me.

Actually, in the beginning of our visit, it *had* been tender and beautiful. And then, as the day wore on, it was as though he just started speaking in clichés. "Don't let anything bother you!" he'd proclaim in this loud voice. It was this slaps-on-the-back kind of talk. It was like he was bluffing happiness, pretending to be happy when he really wasn't. He had changed. Like I said, I had seen Neal change. But usually when Neal and I were together, Neal was still Neal. I saw a tremendous change in Neal, but Neal was still Neal when we were together and we talked. But Jack, when he was drinking at least, became someone I didn't recognize. I wasn't around him often enough in those days to see if it was a superficial thing, just for then—that particular afternoon when he had to deal with me—or if he acted that way all the time. The drinking put on a veneer that didn't let any feelings through, and he wanted it there. I mean, he seemed to be able to handle himself better then. When he was drinking, he could tell people whatever he felt like saying. I don't know. Neal and Jack both changed.

Jack Kerouac in his study, Northport, Long Island, 1964. (Photo by Jerry Bauer.)

The change definitely occurred as he was drinking. I think part of it at least had to be the alcohol. I wasn't around him that much, where I could say, Oh, well, maybe it was just the association of us being together again. I really can't be that good of a judge. But to me it seemed like the alcohol was doing something to his brain. As he continued drinking, he just was dropping all the things that used to make Jack up. And yet something else was going on too. I know that, being there with me, feelings were being dredged up again, and memories of happier times.

In the beginning, in the early afternoon, it was almost like going back in time with him. Like when we were down in Algiers visiting Burroughs, we went over to New Orleans together. I don't know what happened to Neal. But Jack and I had been smoking some pot, and it was also early afternoon. Jack and I were laying on some grass, and we were looking up at the clouds. You know how, when you were a kid, you would see things in the clouds? We must've laid there for three hours, telling each other all of the things we saw in the clouds. We had like three hours of fantastic conversation, just sharing our imaginations with one another. "Do you see this over there?" I'd say, and then he'd say, "Do you see that?" And I would see something over there that related to what he saw. It just went on and on like that. But later on, when we went to Golden Gate Park in San Francisco that afternoon and we both laid down—we were sitting down together, but we both finally laid back—and Jack was holding my hand, we started talking and remembering, just kind of being together. Then, for some reason, he brought up that afternoon in New Orleans, and he talked about seeing things in the clouds. *And he said, "I don't see anything in the clouds anymore."*

He wasn't just talking about the sky in Golden Gate Park that day. He made it very plain that he was telling me about a big change in his life. He said, "I have seen nothing in the clouds anymore—absolutely nothing." He had been through so many years when nobody was publishing his books, when he had no money and his mother had to continue to support him. He was continually being rejected; the publishers were telling him his writings were no good. He'd gone through so many years of scraping and struggling. Under those circumstances, it's hard to keep up your belief in yourself. Because he did have a lot of belief in himself—he really did. But there was a big change in Jack in those years, and the struggles must have taken a hell of a lot out of him. I wanted to just put my arms around him and tell him, "You know, it's all going to be okay now." But he made it such a way that I couldn't have done that. I mean, maybe he was letting me know: "Don't." Maybe he couldn't have handled that kind of thing at that time. I don't know. Because I sure wanted to—I wanted to get close and talk to him.

It was really kind of obvious that Jack wanted somebody to love him and to comfort him. And yet on the other hand, he didn't. He was holding you off with one arm and kind of reaching out with the other, so to speak. It's difficult to really try to analyze someone's feelings when you haven't seen them in a long time, and you don't know all the things that have been happening to them and you don't know exactly where they're coming from. You try to guess what they mean by certain little remarks. But like I said, with Neal I never had to do that. No matter how much he changed, we were always able to talk. But with Jack, it wasn't that way. Maybe he just didn't want the feelings dredged up—and the memories.

In a way, Jack's long slide down, his loss of happiness, started with Neal's rejection in San Francisco in 1949. And then the thing with us fell apart, and all his publishing hopes fell apart too. It was like a snowball. *He had such fantastic expectations!* And then it seemed like everything good that he was anticipating was just kind of being dumped by the way. He was probably starting to think back on things in his life, and it seemed like every time he turned around someone was handing him some kind of rejection slip. By the time *On the Road* became a success, he was already broken inside, and he couldn't handle it. In my view, the fact that he was falling apart emotionally had a great deal to do with his mother. Jack became emotionally dependent on other people, just as he was emotionally dependent on her; and when all those disappointments came, they

GERALD NICOSIA & ANNE MARIE SANTOS

were chipping away at his self-confidence, and really taking such a toll that he didn't realize it himself.

I think he must have felt that he handled all those disappointments all right at the time. But the dependency on his mother shows that he was relying on somebody else to give him strength. He needed her to take care of him. When publication, success, and fame all came, everything he'd anticipated and waited for, all the emotional letdown that he'd already gone through had worn him down and he couldn't accept it. That was it. He didn't have that much left, I don't think, to really go on with his career. Because it is an emotional thing, the fame and people adoring you and hanging on you and complimenting you—this takes an emotional drain on a person also. And I don't think Jack really had that much left to give. It takes strength to survive that kind of success. He had virtually no emotional strength left.

It's strange, I see such a line between Neal and Jack—a line tying them together. I really believe there was something of an umbilical cord between the two of them, because their lives were so entwined, and they really both ran the same gamut, and wound up at the same place. Maybe they were not on exactly the same track, but Neal ran through a lot of the same experiences that Jack did—the emotional drain of being the center of attention, the person everyone looked at. Just like Jack, Neal gave to other people all the time—especially after he was given this thing, the identity of "Dean Moriarty," that he felt he had to keep up. Jack gave through his writing, and Neal gave through being the person Jack wrote about. To me, it was like they were both on the same damn train, and they both gave up at about the same time. I don't think Jack ever felt like the performer, although in the end he became a performer. I think it started in the late 1950s, when they put him on all those TV shows after *On the Road* came out. But it's strange how closely their lives ran.

{ 154 }

Jack Kerouac sharing bottle of Tokay and reading poetry from breast pocket notebook with painter William Morris, San Francisco railyards, 1960. (Photo by James Oliver Mitchell.)

I felt Jack wanted to be like Neal in a lot of ways, but let me make this clear: I never, never found Jack trying to imitate Neal in any way. I used to get a little irritated with Jack because he would always follow Neal—he would do whatever Neal told him to.

No matter what Neal decided, Jack was ready to go—Jack wouldn't ever object to anything Neal wanted to do. Even when I knew or I sensed Jack would feel something wasn't for him, or wasn't what he wanted, he would always allow Neal to take the initiative. That was the only thing that bothered me about their relationship. I never felt that Jack emulated Neal in any way, or tried to, or even wanted to. I mean, he might have wanted to be like Neal, but he would never set himself the goal of trying to make that happen. In the first place, I don't think Jack had enough self-confidence to feel that he could do that, to be very honest with you. But I did hear stories about Jack later in his life, when he was drinking so heavily, that he would be talking nonstop with everybody he met. When Jack was young, when I knew him, he was extremely quiet—he'd sit and listen to others and not talk much himself. But when he became a performer, he had to start talking. And of course—and I'm saying this without having seen him in those years—it wouldn't surprise me if he had started emulating Neal through his alcoholism, with the courage he got from being drunk.

I saw Jack a couple of times on TV, performing, which blew my mind. It was so unlike him—unlike the Jack I knew—that it wasn't real. I couldn't believe that was Jack. I mean, to me it *wasn't* Jack, that's all. I saw him on the Buckley show, *Firing Line*, in 1968—the one where Allen Ginsberg was in the audience. He acted like he didn't recognize Allen as his friend. It was just not Jack—that's all there was to it. I mean, it could have been somebody from Mars, as far as I was concerned. That was no more Jack there than it was anybody else I would have called my friend. I often wondered, after I stopped seeing him, and people were telling me things, or I'd read articles about him, how Jack had become this kind of right-wing bigot, this terrible, angry redneck. *Was he really like that?* I wondered. I would like very much to have talked with him then. I wonder if he was like that when he was sober. But then I've heard he was never sober anymore for the last three or four years of his life—that it was constant drinking.

You see, both of them were desperately trying to get out of it, one way or another—get out of the roles they'd been forced to play. And eventually just to get out of life itself. I felt from Neal, and the things I read about Jack, and the things I saw, that both of them were just hell-bent to destroy themselves. They just were miserable—they were. They wanted to let go, and they both took their own way of doing it, but they were trying to rush it. They were trying like hell just to get out of the whole situation. They just wanted out.

But I hadn't sensed any of that, in Jack at least, until I saw him in California in 1957. Before that, as far as self-destructiveness, I had sensed absolutely none. On the contrary, I always sensed an eager-ness in Jack, almost a little-boy quality of "What's around the next corner?" He was always eager to see the things that his friends were going to do, to see what would happen next. There was absolutely nothing of that kind of darkness in him then. He seemed like the least likely guy to destroy himself. I could never have imagined it. If anyone had told me, in the forties and even in the early fifties, that Jack would become the way he was in the sixties, I would have fought to the death insisting that they were insane. I would have been sure that they didn't know him—that they were just making up nonsense about him. It would have been obvious to me: they could not know him, or they wouldn't say such a thing.

There might have been other people around that were playing death games, like that guy Bill Cannastra who killed himself in the subway, but Jack was always looking for life, always looking for something. He was always eager for what was new. And something turned that around. I think that Neal's death escalated it.* He couldn't accept that Neal was dead. He would tell people that Neal was hiding out from Carolyn—that he didn't want to pay alimony. If he had accepted Neal's death, he would have had to confront what he was doing to himself. They went on a hell-bent mission together, but it's strange how they both took the same road in the end. I mean, there might have been various byways and everything, but they still were on the same damn road. And who could ever have predicted that in the forties, when both of them were so full of hope and anticipation and promise—and their futures, both of them, were bright?

Even for Neal—Neal's success in life wasn't as sure as Jack's. His star might not have been shining as brightly as Jack's, but it was there. Neal would have had absolutely no trouble handling the work at Columbia, if he had ever managed to get admitted. Neal had a fantastic mind, he really did. And his mind was going in the right direction too; his life wasn't wasteful then. But once Neal came to San Francisco and settled down with Carolyn, I never heard him talk anymore about making something of himself. After we came back to California from Denver, I never heard Neal talk any more about his writing or his future or getting an education. I never heard any more of that at all. And that was all he talked about for the four years that I knew him before that. When I first came to San Francisco, in November of 1947, Neal was working at a filling station. He used to make me come out there and sit with him for his eight-hour shift, and he was still talking then about going to school and becoming a

---

* Neal was found unconscious beside some railroad tracks, his body unclothed, his blood filled with downers and alcohol, in San Miguel de Allende, Mexico, in February 1968. He was pronounced dead from exposure a few hours later.

writer. He was still full of anticipation and plans. But then Carolyn got pregnant, and we had to make that trip to Denver just before my eighteenth birthday to get an annulment, so that he could come back and marry her. After we came back from Denver, I never once heard him talk about his old dreams.

Years later, when we were both a lot older, we discussed this—discussed what had happened to his dreams. He said, "Well, you know, I had a responsibility then." Although Neal and responsibility didn't always go hand in hand, Neal felt it greatly. Regardless of what other people have thought, or anything else people have said or written about him, Neal did feel a *big* sense of responsibility! A lot of those things they say about him make me angry. Being raised the way Neal was, Neal hadn't been given a big sense of security—he didn't have a lot to work from. He didn't really know how to handle responsibility because *no one had ever been responsible for him.* And the only one he'd ever had to be responsible for was himself. But he still tried to be responsible, when he could. Even with me, he did the best he could. He was always very gentle with me and tried to make everything nice for me, because he felt I had been short-changed by being on my own so young. He knew I wasn't prepared for life on my own, the way I had been raised—which was always a proper and protected environment. So he felt a sense of responsibility toward me, but at the same time he felt sure I could learn to take care of myself—that I could make it on my own if he gave me a little help in that direction.

Neal had a large sense of responsibility, or he would never have married Carolyn. He would never have married Diana either. He would never have gone through the whole bullshit of annulments and divorces just so he could keep getting remarried and taking care of his different families. And he would never have even tried to get Carolyn alimony at various times when she told him that she and the kids were desperate for money. He was always really *worried* about her and the kids. He really tried to help them out. I know that, especially in the earlier years, Carolyn thought that Neal could have cared less whether they were eating or had a roof over their heads. The truth is, he really was concerned. Unfortunately, he just didn't know what to do about it, but he felt it greatly.

In a way, he was just like Jack with his emotional dependency thing with the women. Look at what happened with Joan.* When Jack was with a woman he cared about, I think he would love to have been in the traditional role of husband and father; he would love to have been able to take over the reins and do the things that he knew might have to be done, or should be done, to take care of his family. But since all these things had been done for him all his life—and done by a woman, his mother—he really had no way of knowing how to do it. Jack's mother had made him dependent on her, and it made him helpless in a lot of ways. It was the same with Neal in that respect. He didn't have a mother making him dependent, but he had nobody giving him a responsible model either. Neal really wanted desperately to take care of his responsibilities, and live up to them, and he just really didn't know how to go about it.

Jack used to talk about how "the place for a woman is handling the money." He really felt that way—that the woman should take care of the practical things in life. With Neal, because of his upbringing on skid row, where you had to fight to protect whatever belongings you had—with Neal, it was always a "This is yours, and this is mine!" type of thing. It was hard for him to feel a togetherness thing with anyone—to really open up and share with anyone.

---

* Joan Haverty was Jack's second wife. They married in November 1950; but when she got pregnant a few months later, Jack abandoned her, refused to admit paternity of her daughter, Janet Michelle, and refused to pay child support until he was compelled to do so by a court of law.

I mean, we had a tremendous togetherness; but from a material standpoint, Neal didn't even begin to understand what it might mean to say the word *ours*. If he had five bucks in his pocket, it was his five bucks! And he needed it. If Jack had five bucks, of course, it was his mother's five bucks.

The funny thing is, they were both nearly broke when they died. In their last years, they were barely able to take care of even themselves. Jack couldn't pay his bills, and Neal was simply living off of others. From all the conversations that Neal and I had through the years, I think Neal was a little resentful as he grew older—not resentful of people, but just of circumstances, the circumstances that placed him where he landed. He ended up being kind of half-assed famous, but for nothing he had done—at least nothing he was proud of having done. It was not like he had a profession he could be proud of, or any way to earn a living. They even took away his job on the railroad.* Especially toward the end of his life, like when he was with Kesey, he began to grow very bitter.**

He sometimes drove over to my house with the bus, and one time we spent a couple of weeks together down the Peninsula, close to Los Gatos. A friend of Neal's, John Gourley, had a cabin down there. When Neal used to get tired, those were usually the times he'd come and see me and we'd go away together. And he would just kind of let down with me. One of those times, he was telling me about his

---

* Neal had been arrested in 1958 for handing two narcotics agents three marijuana cigarettes in exchange for a ride to the train station one morning. As a result, he received a felony conviction for both possessing and dealing marijuana, and served two years in the California state penitentiary at San Quentin. After his release, he was not allowed to return to his job on the Southern Pacific Railroad.

** In the early 1960s, Cassady joined the countercultural band called The Merry Pranksters, which was led by novelist Ken Kesey and based at La Honda, California. The Pranksters rode around the country in a psychedelically painted old school bus dubbed "Furthur," and Neal became their celebrated driver, as well as a sort of mascot for the entire group.

"throwing the hammer" bit.[*] It's strange, because he had never done it in front of me—almost as if he was ashamed to actually let me see it. A lot of people had told me about it. They said it was frightening to watch him, because it seemed like he would never stop. But now Neal was telling me about it himself. He talked about it like he was a performing monkey. He said something like, "I put on my act at six o'clock and eight o'clock."

One day I happened to be down at the warehouse where the bus and everyone was staying. Neal and I were having one of our heart-to-heart talks, when he got a call from Kesey. Some show on KPIX was doing an interview with Kesey, and Ken wanted Neal to come down to KPIX and be part of the show.[**] Neal asked me to come with him—maybe for moral support. It was like being with someone who was a professional performer. Our conversation completely stopped when Kesey called him. On went the pink satin shirt, and he just completely went into an act. It was as though he instantly became someone else. It was like there were two Neals. I was talking to one person one minute—to *Neal*—and the next minute he was a different person, a stranger in a pink satin shirt with a sledgehammer in his hand.

There were periods in the late sixties when I didn't see Neal for a long time. The last time I saw him was in the fall of 1967. This was just before he went down to Mexico, on that trip he wouldn't come back from. The period before that visit, he had been gone from the Bay Area for quite a while. I think it had been a year probably since I had last seen him. He was getting very tired at that point. He met me at the restaurant right down at the corner near my house in Daly City. He had that small minibus that the Pranksters used to

---

[*] Cassady was one of the Pranksters' star attractions, and people would come from far and wide to see him tossing a small sledgehammer up into the air and flawlessly catching it, over and over, sometimes for hours at a stretch.

[**] KPIX is a San Francisco television station.

get around in when they weren't driving the big bus. He told me he had been down to see his daughter Cathy's first child—I think they were living in Texas—and it was as though he were relieved that he had gotten this accomplished. I mean, he talked totally unlike Neal. Even at periods like when Natalie had committed suicide, and even when he was really down, Neal had never talked the way he talked that day. It was as though—and I later told Allen Ginsberg this—it was as though he was just tired of his whole life. And he asked me, *"Where do we go from here, Babe?"*

He couldn't connect with me the way he had in the past. I can't quite describe the way he was, because Neal had never been like that before. He was extremely quiet, for one thing. He wasn't talking. He was so down that he really didn't have anything to say. Then he told me he was going to Mexico, but he had to go up north first, to Oregon—or he had been to Oregon, I can't remember now. But it was as though he was saying, "I'm tired of the whole fucking mess—it just isn't worth it anymore." I told Al Hinkle about this too. This was long before I heard about Neal dying in Mexico. I was in the hospital when he passed away. It was as though he was through. He just didn't want any part of life anymore. He didn't want anything anymore. The only thing he was relieved about was seeing his grandson, his first grandchild. He said, "I at least did that. I at least got down there to see her baby." Cathy was kind of special to him. Well, she was his first kid—at least the first one that he raised, that he acted as a father toward. He'd heard that she was about to have a baby, and he raced down there—got down there while she was still in the hospital. It was something that meant a great deal to him, that he felt he had to do. He was very relieved that he had done it—as if this was one thing that he had finally done right with his life.

The fact that Neal had become a performer at the end—it was so unlike him, so completely, totally unlike him. It was even unlike the

Neal that all these writers had written about in their books. Even though Neal was a mover, a doer, he was always doing things for himself—doing things he had chosen to do. I mean, his *thought* was the thing about him that got us all so excited. What was remarkable was the fact that he was interested in so many things. Like Al and I were talking about recently, when we were kids, Neal could be reading a book and shooting pool and necking with me at the same time—*and giving his attention to all three.* But those were things that he wanted to do. He wasn't putting on a show; he wasn't trying to impress anyone. He could've cared less if anyone even noticed. That wasn't the case in later years.

It was that change that bothered him. When we would be together, we would talk about the things that might have been, the things that had happened and changed everything. He felt, I think, cheated. I mean, he didn't blame anyone. He blamed himself more than anyone else. Neal was his own worst critic in that respect. He was angry at himself that he hadn't gone ahead and pursued his dreams. Because even when we were first married, Neal would type and write on into the night—whether he would have turned into a great writer, who knows? In those days, of course, he wasn't into whether anyone was ever going to read his work or not. But he wanted to write, and he wanted to go to school. He wanted the education so that he would be able to do it and do it right. Whether or not he had the talent is something we'll probably never know. A few years ago, City Lights published *The First Third*. He wrote that, my God, a hundred years ago—but he never finished it. It was unfinished, like his whole life.

Nowadays so many people want to write about us. They want to know every detail of our lives. What makes me sad is that they don't want to know *why* we did the things we did. We were poor, but we made do the best we could. We tried to keep clean, to be neat. We had purposes and plans, just like everyone does.

Neal Cassady, San Francisco, 1963. (Photo by Larry Keenan, Jr.)

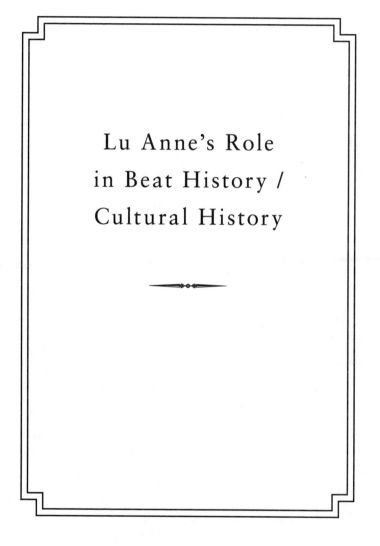

Lu Anne's Role
in Beat History /
Cultural History

With a few exceptions, like Tom Christopher's well-researched but still unfinished tabloid-format biography of Neal Cassady,* portraits of Lu Anne in Beat histories tend to be extremely reductive, not to say demeaning. William Plummer, in the first biography of Cassady, *The Holy Goof*, refers to her as "a scarcely domesticated barbarian."** The most flattering portraits of her are as a teenage sex bomb with blonde ringlets down to her waist—and her chief value and raison d'être seems to be as proof of Neal Cassady's power over women. It's as if she's dragged out on the Beat stage so people can say, "Look at this man's sexual prowess! He could get a woman this desirable and make her do his every bidding, put up with his every infidelity. He must've been quite a man!" Few of these chroniclers have evinced any interest in what ideas the lady might

---

* Titled simply *Neal Cassady*, and self-published in Vashon, Washington, in 1998.
** William Plummer, *The Holy Goof: A Biography of Neal Cassady* (New York: Paragon paperback edition, 1990), p. 44.

have had in her own head; and fewer still have asked whether she might have been on some quests of her own. No one, that I know of, has ever pointed out, *She must have been quite a woman to get this interesting and fabled guy to keep coming back to her, all his life—right up to the moment when he left for Mexico and the death he seems to have foreseen coming.*

When Neal Cassady told her, "You are my one and only wife," he was recognizing something in her that droves of subsequent biographers and annotators have failed to notice: that Lu Anne Henderson Cassady played a unique and irreplaceable role in that great man's life, and hence, by extension, in all the lives he touched, which were some significant lives indeed. She was not a fungible commodity, not just one more instance of the teenage pussy—"young stuff in filmy sheer no underclothes dresses," as he described his dream girls in a letter to Jack—of which he seemed able to gather an inexhaustible store. She was the impetus and sine qua non of a change in Neal Cassady that allowed him to become *the* Neal Cassady we know today, the prototype of so many rebel and outlaw clichés, and the begetter of the Beat Generation itself.

It is pretty well accepted that there would have been no Beat Generation had Jack Kerouac not met Neal Cassady. But along with that justifiable assumption there usually comes another tacit one, not really justified at all: that once Neal met Jack, it was like the sperm meeting the egg—that after the conception, it was only a matter of time before the embryo matured and the Beat Generation was born. The fact is, Neal meeting Jack was not enough to have created one of the most important literary, social, and cultural movements of the twentieth century. When they met—as Lu Anne tells eloquently in her interview—they didn't even like each other, and they certainly didn't understand each other.

From vastly different backgrounds—Neal having been orphaned

from any real sense of family or social position almost from his birth, while Jack was steeped in family to his very bones, and sought every sort of conventional validation, from school to sports to a useful role in society, and more—it was almost preordained that they would not trust each other at all, and, moreover, they had no basis for building that trust. Mutual friendship with two or three guys like Hal Chase and Ed White would not have been enough, since Chase and White barely trusted Neal themselves. There needed to be a very special key that would unlock Neal and Jack's hearts toward each other, and that key was Lu Anne Henderson.

What gave the Beat Generation so much potency was its embodiment and unification—in a harmony that would previously have been thought impossible—of great opposites. The postwar period—the late 1940s and early 1950s—was arguably the most polarized period in American history. One was either a Communist or a democratic American, a churchgoer or an atheist, a practicer of marital fidelity or a promiscuous sex fiend. It was all either-ors, no in-betweens. The founders of the Beat Generation were, above all, seekers of gradations, explorers of the possible gray areas of human life. Kerouac and Cassady were, at the start, too far apart to bring each other the new possibilities that they eventually offered in the way of expanded humanity. It was Lu Anne who saw their similarities—who saw their heart, their caring, their desire to do good across the old boundaries and deep into a new world where the old values just didn't make sense anymore. She coaxed and cajoled and argued them into accepting and valuing each other; she almost single-handedly brought them together into a deep friendship. That may seem like an extreme statement, and there may be no way of proving it. But I'd bet money on it if I could.

The fact is, when Jack and Neal first met, they had trouble talking to each other—this has been well-documented in the observations of many friends—beyond simply comparing their achievements: how far they could pass a football, how many books they'd read, how many Lester Young and Coleman Hawkins songs they knew by heart, and so forth. But each of them had long, soulful talks with Lu Anne. She was, among other things, one of the world's great listeners. They both told her, separately, their most intimate life stories. She would then share what she'd learned from Neal with Jack, and what she'd learned from Jack with Neal. Their respect for, and trust of, each other began to grow, precisely because they both respected and trusted her.

Although she had little formal education, she had a profound understanding of people—and all those close to her saw it immediately. People, especially Jack and Neal, trusted her judgments. And so she made them both believe that each was worthy of the other's love and concern. It didn't hurt that she also tied them all together in one big love knot. But with or without the shared sexual bonds, she was a powerful cement that held them together. And the nature of that cement was precisely the goodness and honesty she brought to every relationship. Her love for Neal made Jack see, and *believe in*, things he had never suspected in Neal earlier; and ditto for Neal with Jack. Furthermore, she made them see that they loved each other equally—that each one's love and respect for the other was fully reciprocated—something both men doubted for a long time. But when Lu Anne told them it was so, they had to believe it.

Lu Anne brought Neal and Jack close enough for the nuclear fusion to finally occur—and with it, the explosion that changed life in America forever. Neal's relentless action joined with Jack's endless weighing of possibilities, Jack's dawdling over details with Neal's speedy pursuit of the macrodestination; Jack's excessive Catholic conscience joined with Neal's forced pragmatism of a homeless street kid; Jack's rigid (but often sharp and canny) working-class politics and political categories joined with Neal's apolitical pursuit of the greatest common good; and Jack's belief in a personal God in the clouds joined with Neal's homegrown pantheism, his belief that God was as much in a car's gears or a woman's thighs as in any traditional religious heaven.

While all of these assertions can be argued or contested, there can be no doubt that the overall impact of two such very different men joining forces, and *joining consciousnesses*—or as poet Michael McClure would later put it, joining their respective *sensoriums*—especially since that union was so well-documented in books like *On the Road*, *Go*, and other ongoing discourse and legend of the time, created at least one of the viable starting points for all the seismic social and cultural shifts of the sixties and later decades. The beatniks were born; the hippies were born on their heels; and after the short stutter step of the early seventies, the punks were born. All owed a huge debt to the coming together of Kerouac and Cassady, the confluence of those two very different energies. And the coming together of Kerouac and Cassady owed a great debt to Lu Anne Henderson. Who says one person can't profoundly change the human universe?

That Lu Anne's role has remained so largely unacknowledged is due to many things. One could spend a whole essay on the media's proclivity for male over female heroes. Once they had Kerouac and Cassady as figureheads of countercultural dissent and dissatisfaction, why should they muddle the snappy narrative by introducing a woman's role into the story? But I think we need to look further, into the fact that Lu Anne was a deeply troubled person, barely able to keep her head above water—keep herself in the world of the living—let alone try to leave her mark on the culture by writing books or creating a public persona, as Kerouac did.

For that matter, would a character as troubled as Cassady ever have managed to leave his mark without the dozens of hardworking, and for the most part far more survival-oriented, artists (including Kerouac, Holmes, Kesey, even Tom Wolfe) who turned his life into the durable artifacts of printed articles, books, photographs, and film? In that respect, as Neal claimed, Lu Anne was too much like himself. In the one letter to him that survives, she speaks of how difficult it is for her to get through the intense "torment" she sometimes experienced. She had broken too many barriers—gone too far out into unexplored territory—and there was no safety zone for her to retreat to. She was forced to keep going forward with her life, but as marriage after marriage, and dream after dream, failed, she had no idea where she was going. As she reports in her long interview, Neal asked her near the end of his life, "Where do we go from here, Babe?"—doubtless aware that she was then as hopelessly adrift as he.

But in going so far out, she was pioneering new roles for a woman, for women's sexuality and personal freedom—though nobody, to my knowledge, has acknowledged her as a precursor to Friedan, Steinem, and the feminist movement that came along two decades later. For a "decent" middle-class young woman of the mid-1940s, it was unthinkable to fall in love with—let alone run away with, steal for, break a host of laws for—a wild, homeless, lower-class, convicted criminal, as Neal Cassady was when she met and married him. Then to go on, not only to accept his promiscuous sexuality (which was something women were often forced to do in those days) but to welcome multiple sexual partners herself, put her in a social Coventry that would have seemed beyond redemption in post-World War II America.

But far from feeling shamed, humiliated, doomed, etc., as she was supposed to—according to the tenets of American society at the time—she was glad of her life, she loved her life, she loved all the people in her life, she rejoiced in the ever-widening spectrum of experience that came her way. And she did not shy from the notion—which terrified so many people back then—that it is possible to love more than one person at a time. Lu Anne sought to love as many people as she could—whether sexually or platonically did not seem a significant difference to her. Love was love to her, and each person brought a new richness to her life that she ardently desired and forever treasured. Men had been taking that approach since the dawn of time, but until then it had been unthinkable for a woman—to use the words of Thoreau—to demand such a "broad margin" to her life, to declare that she had as much right to go through every open door as a man had.

Lu Anne was mostly uneducated, and so she did not embark upon all these revolutionary behaviors with some sort of theoretical underpinning or philosophical framework to guide her actions—nor did she aim to share her experiences in a way that would influence the behavior of other women. There was, after all, no feminist movement at the time that she could join or see herself as part of. But she was not ashamed of her actions either; and although she wanted to "call" Kerouac on some of the distortions of her life that she felt he put into *On the Road*, she never regretted his making the essence of her life public in print, and known to the world. Nor did she ever recant or apologize for her unconventional life. In some ways, it's true, she tried to raise her daughter to a more conventional life than the one she herself had led, but that was mainly to shield Annie from some of the pains and problems—not to say near debacles—that she herself had experienced. She also, eventually, told Annie the full details of her past life—told them with great humor and in a way that would allow Annie to benefit from all the revolutionary dues Lu Anne had had to pay to ride, not just in the vanguard of the Beats, but in the vanguard of new role models for women of the late twentieth century.

Lu Anne, her mother Thelma, and her husband Sam Catechi, at club owned by Sam, San Francisco, 1953. (Photo courtesy of Anne Marie Santos.)

One final question that might be asked, I suppose, is if—or to what extent—Lu Anne realized the revolutionary role she played on the twentieth-century American stage. Having spent only two days, and less than a dozen hours total, with Lu Anne, I may not be the best person to answer this. But I can honestly say that the dignity and self-worth she radiated—as strongly as the warm sunshine of her smile—were far beyond that of the ordinary homemaker of Daly City, California. You could not be with her more than a few minutes without feeling as if you were with someone special, and someone who was well aware of how special she was.

That she was known to, and respected by, people from all walks of life—everyone from the mayor of San Francisco to rock promoter Bill Graham—as her daughter reports, is significant testimony to the evident power she felt in herself and reflected to others. For, I believe, others could not have recognized Lu Anne's unique character if she did not recognize it, and wear it comfortably, herself. It is significant that many of the important people she impressed, whether a singer like Johnny Mathis or a topless dancer like Carol Doda, did not know her specifically as "Marylou" of *On the Road*, though they might have known her as a strikingly independent woman in some other capacity, such as North Beach club owner or power broker in the city's underground politics.

To me, it was also significant that she expressed such a strong longing to get back in touch with some of the major artists she had once mingled so easily with—often asking me what had become of people whose names came up in the course of the interview, or, as in the case of John Holmes, asking me to send along her best regards to him. It was clear she missed her days closer to the center of artistic creation, visionary exploration, and cultural change. There was also a touch of sadness I would see in her eyes or hear in her voice, from time to time, as she probably realized the almost insurmountable obstacles that now lay between her and the kind of freedom and significance her life had once had.

A final fact that convinces me that Lu Anne knew who she was, and at least glimpsed the grandeur of her own accomplishments, was the way she reacted to the movies that were being made about her. She was angry that *Heart Beat* had caught only the superficial aspects of her rebellion—and had reduced her choice to love freely, across all the moral boundaries of the day, to a decision to live with poor hygiene. By the same token, she told her daughter that she was greatly looking forward to, and held high hopes for, the new film that would be made of *On the Road*, and hence of her early life, by Walter Salles, a director known for his respectful treatment of political and cultural revolutionaries. It is one further, sad irony of Lu Anne's life that she died so shortly before that film finally went into production.

One can but hope that actress Kristen Stewart, who got to listen to Lu Anne's taped interview and to talk extensively with her daughter, Annie, before playing the role of Lu Anne on camera, will finally give the great courage and innovative spirit, as well as the vast heart of this woman, their long-deferred due.

Kristen Stewart and Walter Salles at Beat Boot Camp, Montreal, July 2010. Kristen is listening to Lu Anne's tapes. (Photo by Gerald Nicosia.)

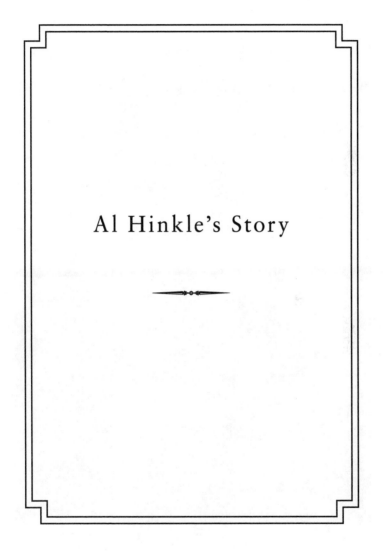

Al Hinkle's Story

Al Hinkle, circa 1946, the year he reconnected with Neal Cassady. (Photo courtesy of Al Hinkle.)

A l Hinkle was probably Neal Cassady's best friend. In *On the Road*, he is portrayed as Big Ed Dunkel, the extraordinarily faithful sidekick and helper who will do anything for Neal, even abandon his new wife (Helen) a quarter way across the continent, so that they can get to North Carolina and Neal's other good buddy, Jack Kerouac, a little quicker and with a little less hassle.

Born in the same year, 1926, Neal and Al met in Denver when they were both 13 and performed together in a YMCA circus. They did a high-wire-and-trapeze act together—with a net under them—and Neal, ever the athlete, was the one to fly across, somersaulting in midair, while Al, who was a lot taller than Neal, was the one waiting on the other side to catch him. A few years later, in 1946, they met again through a mutual friend, the gimpy, bug-eyed pool hustler Jimmy Holmes, down at Pederson's Pool Hall. As soon as Neal, who as usual was drifting with no job, no money, and often no place to sleep, learned that Al had both a job and his own car, a 1936 straight-8 LaSalle convertible, Neal glommed on to Al as the guy who could put him behind a wheel (something he desired prob-ably more than beautiful young women) and provide him with the one absolutely vital component of his life: mobility.

In fact, the day they remet at the pool hall, now both 20, Neal asked Al to let him drive the LaSalle down to the local drive-in restau-rant on Spears Boulevard, where his wife was working as a carhop. Al was amazed to hear that the handsome but ne'er-do-well, penni-less Cassady actually had a wife, but he was even more astounded when he saw Lu Anne come running out to them in her frilly carhop's uniform, complete with low-cut blouse and ultra-short skirt that showed off her long, perfect legs. Her blonde hair was long too, and her skin strikingly pale. Lu Anne Cassady was the most beautiful woman Al had seen up till then, but Cassady casually kissed her as if having this gorgeous 16-year-old heartthrob gush all over him was no big deal. He never even bothered to get out of the car; he had her bring them Cokes. Then Neal turned the car around and headed back to Pederson's Pool Hall, where Al got yet another shock.

A few minutes after they got back, two young women walked in from the alley—one of them Al recognized from junior high school, a barely pretty blonde with stringy hair and an aggressive attitude named Jeannie Stewart. "Oh, this's my girlfriend Jeannie," Neal explained. It turned out Neal was living at her house, a circum-stance he explained as being due to his inability to rent a place for himself and Lu Anne. Whenever Lu Anne saved up a couple of bucks from her carhop tips, Neal would later tell Al, they rented a room (with no bath) for the night at the nearby Trentham Arms flophouse. Al would also soon learn that Neal was not only living with, and having sex regularly with, Jeannie, but he was also having regular sex with Jeannie's mother and grandmother, who lived in the same house—and who demanded Neal's servicing as a condition for allowing him to stay there.

It was to finally pry Neal away from Jeannie, according to Al, that Lu Anne insisted they leave Denver together and go live with her aunt and uncle in Nebraska—the moment in the story where her long interview printed in this volume begins.

Al would subsequently have hundreds of adventures with both Neal and Lu Anne, and eventually become the confidant of both as well. He remained friends with both of them until their respective deaths, Neal's in 1968 and Lu Anne's in 2010. He probably knew more about them than anyone on the planet—and certainly knew more about them even than they knew about each other.

Al paints a picture of Lu Anne as a smart and very pretty girl, shuffled around by divorced parents busy trying to survive the Great Depression—a girl who became sexually active very early. Although Al admits he cannot verify all the things he heard about Lu Anne, he feels fairly sure that the reason her father sent her back from Los Angeles to her mother in Denver, when Lu Anne was only 12, was that his daughter had been "growing up too fast" in L.A. and had already become, or was close to becoming, sexually involved with an older guy. Al also learned that the reason Lu Anne's mom agreed to let her marry Cassady was that Lu Anne's stepfather was pressuring her to have sex with him. Lu Anne later admitted as much to Cassady biographer Tom Christopher. Lu Anne had been deeply troubled by her stepfather's advances, but it wasn't due to any sexual naiveté or inhibitions on her part. Al relates that at 14, Lu Anne and her girlfriend Lois had already been getting "presents" from a well-to-do Denver storekeeper, in exchange for sexual favors, including oral sex, in the back room of his store. He says Lu Anne told him this story herself.

One of the reasons that Al was able to become close to Lu Anne so quickly was that she was already close to his friend Jimmy Holmes. She liked Jimmy as a friend, but he was most important to her as a source of information about her often absent husband. Whenever they'd get together, Jimmy would fill her in on Neal's whereabouts and latest extracurricular activities. Soon Al was going with Jimmy and Lu Anne once or twice a week to movies at the Broadway Theater, and Lu Anne talked freely with the two of them about her life. She knew that Neal was incorrigible in his pursuit of other women, and she had grave doubts about whether the marriage was going to work out. But she loved him, she made clear to Al and Jimmy, and that was why she was hanging in, giving it the best shot she could.

Al tells a surprising version of how Neal met his second wife, Carolyn Robinson, then a graduate student in fine art and theater at the University of Denver. It was the summer of 1947, and Neal and Lu Anne were living together back in Denver after their sojourn in New York half a year earlier. In her book *Off the Road,*[*] Carolyn writes that she had spent most of a day with her boyfriend Bill Tomson and Cassady before meeting Lu Anne, along with Al Hinkle and Lois, in Carolyn's hotel room later that evening. In Carolyn's account, she had developed a strong rapport with Cassady before learning that he was married; then, again by her account, she had to suffer a great deal of cattiness from Lu Anne in her hotel room, where Neal secretly signaled to her that he would return to see her at two in the morning. Carolyn's version is that Neal primly spent the night with her—no sex—and the next morning Lu Anne came over to give Carolyn her permission to date Neal, since she didn't want him anymore.

Hinkle relates that Bill Tomson brought his gang of friends— Hinkle and Lois, Neal and Lu Anne—to meet Carolyn at her hotel

* Carolyn Cassady, *Off the Road: Twenty Years with Cassady, Kerouac and Ginsberg* (London: Black Spring Press, 2007), pp. 1–15.

room. According to Al, Lu Anne saw Neal paying attention to Carolyn, but she didn't get catty about it. Lu Anne didn't particularly like it, but she was used to Neal doing such things. He says Neal did sneak back to rendezvous later with Carolyn, but only stayed briefly—long enough to have sex—and then returned to Lu Anne. Rather than Neal switching his attentions to Carolyn, as she tells the story, Al says that Neal was still focused on trying to live with Lu Anne—and after she could no longer afford to rent her own place, Al let them use his stepfather's empty apartment as a love nest. Interestingly, after Neal left town briefly to take a carpenter's job that didn't pan out, Al recalls Bill Tomson bringing Carolyn by the same empty apartment to bed her there—so Carolyn's break with Bill, after she met Neal, was nowhere near as clear-cut as she has painted it.

Moreover, Al has no recollection of Lu Anne giving Carolyn permission to pursue her husband. Al also remembers Neal telling him around this time that he had a "real connection" with Lu Anne and that he expected they would always be together. What is most interesting about Al's version of the story is the different attitude he ascribes to Lu Anne. According to Al, Lu Anne was not the games-playing, opportunistic skank that Carolyn portrays her as; she was much more the long-suffering, even if only 17-year-old wife, who desperately wanted to keep her husband but didn't know how to deal with his endless roving, and was struggling through trial and error to figure out how much rope to give him.

The picture we get of Lu Anne from Al is of a woman who early on got used to life dealing her bad hands, but who never just lay back and passively took life's slings and arrows, or moped about her troubles—she was always on her feet and going forward, trying to make a way for herself. But she did not try to make her way opportunistically—she always cared about others who were on the journey with her; she always gave more than she took. She had to drop out of high school when she married Neal, but she never complained about giving up her education. She was not afraid of hard work either. Neal, in Hinkle's words, "wasn't too big on working," but Lu Anne was always ready to grab any job she could find, just so they'd have a roof over their heads and food on the table. Most of the time there was nobody, not even family, willing to take care of her.

Al recalls how when she got back to Denver in early 1947, while Neal was still in New York, she asked Al to get her a job at Rocky Built, a burger joint where he worked, so that she could afford a place for her and Neal to live when he returned—and he says that she worked long hours there for several months and used her salary to rent a small hotel room. She was certain he would return to her by June, and he actually returned to Denver just a couple of weeks after she did—though she didn't bargain on Neal meeting Carolyn that summer and all the other madness that followed.

Like a lot of people who have grown up in extreme poverty and been neglected by their family, Lu Anne had learned to bend and break rules, when necessary, to survive. But Hinkle remembers her as a woman with a conscience perhaps too big for her own good. He tells a story of how Neal talked her old boyfriend Don into driving him and Lu Anne to Colorado Springs; and how, on the way back, when Neal was driving and the cops pulled him over for speeding, he and Lu Anne quickly pulled the drunken, groggy Don under the steering wheel so that he'd get the ticket instead of Neal, who had no driver's license. Lu Anne said nothing to the police, to protect Neal, but she felt guilty for years that she'd been to blame for Don's arrest.

Too often she took responsibility for the misdeeds of the men in her life. Partly this self-abnegation and deference toward men seems to have come from her childhood, from the guilt she felt for leaving her real dad in Los Angeles, at about 12 years old, to go live with her mom and new stepfather in Denver. But part of giving men more than they deserved also came, according to Hinkle, from her strong sex drive, her great need to have forceful male lovers in her life, and so she would put up with a lot to keep them. She told Al that no lover ever satisfied her as well as Neal had. But she put up with a lot from her second husband, Ray Murphy, too. She'd vacillated about marrying him—especially when it seemed she might have a chance of connecting permanently with Jack Kerouac—but in the end she felt obligated to marry him because she'd taken his ring and promised him she would. She'd already glimpsed his heavy drinking and violent jealousy, but went ahead with the marriage anyway, blaming herself for Murphy's instability and roughness with her because she had remained too connected to Neal.

Though Murphy sired her only child, Anne Marie (unless we choose to believe Neal's version that *he* was the girl's father), the marriage was otherwise a disaster. Time and again, his jealousy exploded out of control, and he beat Lu Anne mercilessly for offenses which were mostly in his own imagination. Al recalls her showing up at the house on 18th Street and Valencia in San Francisco where he lived with his wife, Helen, only a few months after she'd married Murphy, with her face all puffy and black and blue. She begged him to allow her to spend the night, but refused to point the finger at Murphy for the pummeling she'd received, afraid that Al might go find Murphy and give him a taste of his own medicine.

And Al would not have hesitated to avenge her. He admits that he had long before started to fall in love with her himself. "Her personality stood out as much as her physical beauty," Al recalled, 60 years after she'd crawled into bed with him and his wife, and a year after Lu Anne's death. "She was always so outgoing—so loving, kind, and considerate." His eyes looked a little misty as he recalled how she went back to Murphy against his advice.

And then Murphy came banging on his door the following night. As soon as Al let him in, Murphy lit into Al, accusing him of being a "go-between for Neal and Lu Anne," and threatening to hurt Al if he continued doing this. In truth, Lu Anne was certainly still involved with Neal, but Hinkle had had nothing to do with helping that along. He didn't even know where Lu Anne lived, and Neal had had no trouble finding her on his own. Hinkle told him, "I don't agree with you beating the shit out of your wife," and then offered to go outside with him and settle their differences right then and there. Murphy, he says, looked like a "tough guy," but Al was bigger than Murphy and, since he worked on the railroad, had a few muscles of his own. Murphy, he says, turned in silence and left. Hinkle concluded that "he was a bully who preferred beating up women to fighting with other men."

As the years went by, Hinkle continued to see Lu Anne from time to time. She showed him her baby, Annie Ree (born December 18, 1950), when the girl was about three months old. He recalls that Neal continued to see her, off and on, through the early 1950s—and he maintains that their sexual relationship actually continued sporadically till the end of Neal's life.

But Lu Anne had a number of other boyfriends during this period too. Hinkle remembers one night in particular, in about 1957, when Lu Anne again showed up at his house in the middle of the night, this time with her seven-year-old daughter in tow. She told him she had to meet a guy in Los Angeles, and could she leave Annie Ree with him and his wife for a day or two? Al agreed to help her out, but he grew increasingly concerned as the days, then weeks, passed with no word from Lu Anne. The Hinkles placed Annie Ree in school with their own daughter, Dawn, but Al was virtually in a panic, since he did not know how to contact Lu Anne's two half brothers or anyone else in her family. Finally, about three weeks later, Lu Anne returned

*Lu Anne in her Lilli Ann fitted suit, with her third husband,
Sam Catechi, Little Bohemia club, San Francisco, 1953.
(Photo courtesy of Anne Marie Santos.)*

to pick up her daughter. She was black and blue again. "The guy turned violent" was the only explanation she ever gave Hinkle about that episode.

Over the years, Al said, he often visited with Lu Anne on his day off; or sometimes they'd have lunch, and she would drive him back to the railroad afterward. They often reminisced about Neal, Jack, and the wild times they'd had together. For several years, she worked as a cocktail waitress at San Francisco Airport, making great tips and meeting lots of important people.

Then she surprised Al one day, in about 1953, when she told him about a Greek man named Sam Catechi, a San Francisco nightclub owner whom she'd met while cocktail-waitressing in North Beach. Catechi had quickly proposed marriage, and she'd just as quickly accepted. He was several decades older than she, a dapper guy who looked something like an overweight Clark Gable. In Al's view, he appeared incongruous next to the gorgeous, youthful-looking Lu Anne, who was still getting carded at bars even in her late twenties. Soon after their marriage, Catechi bought her a home in Daly City. Al's take on the marriage was that Lu Anne had sought security for herself and her young daughter, which Catechi gave them. Catechi acted as a father toward Annie Ree, who took his last name, and Lu Anne kept the house even after they divorced two years later. Their parting was amiable, and Lu Anne appeared to feel gratitude toward him for more than just his financial support. She told Hinkle she'd learned a sophistication from Catechi that she'd never had before.

Lu Anne's fourth husband, Bob Skonecki, came along in 1960, and she married him in 1963. He was another merchant seaman, the sort of big, handsome, muscular guy who was much more her type. But like Murphy, he was away at sea for long periods; and there were new, troublesome factors in her life—including serious failings of her health—that kept their marriage from being just a happy ride into the sunset together.

Around 1953, perhaps through her connection to Sam Catechi and his Little Bohemia club, Lu Anne met another San Francisco club owner named Joe DeSanti. A powerful figure, with five clubs in the Barbary Coast and North Beach, DeSanti was romantically drawn to Lu Anne, but their affair didn't last long. For whatever reason, he wasn't her ideal lover; but eventually the relationship grew into a very close friendship—she often described them as like a brother and sister, looking out for each other and taking care of each other whenever necessary. At that time, Lu Anne was already growing seriously debilitated from irritable bowel syndrome (IBS), which she'd suffered from since childhood. With Lu Anne's health growing ever more problematic, she clearly needed someone she could rely on during bouts of illness or in other troubled times.

DeSanti became a kind of de facto godfather to Annie Ree as well. He even bought a house only a few blocks from Lu Anne's in Daly City. When Joe went to jail for two or three years on a federal tax evasion charge, he asked Lu Anne to manage one of his North Beach nightclubs for him.

DeSanti's club was on Broadway, right in the middle of the North Beach strip, and those years when Lu Anne ran it, 1959 to 1961, opened up a new world to her. The group of San Francisco club owners and entertainers were a close-knit community, and in this small world she met people like future superpromoter Bill Graham, who often frequented Basin Street West, where everyone from Lenny Bruce to Smokey Robinson and the Miracles performed; the political glad-hander George Moscone, who would become one of the city's most famous, and later tragic, mayors; and local songster Johnny Mathis, the golden-voiced alumnus (and former star athlete) of San Francisco's George Washington High School, whom Joe turned down after an audition at his club, thinking the kid didn't show much promise, but who got work soon after at the Jazz Workshop next door. Lu Anne liked the experience so much that when Joe got out of jail, she went on—possibly with DeSanti's or Catechi's help—to buy her own club on Broadway, the Pink Elephant, which she personally ran from 1961 to 1963. Her daughter remembers Lu Anne's years managing that nightclub as some of the happiest of her life—mingling with all sorts of celebrities and powerful people, as well as getting to assert her independence and show off her management and people skills, which were considerable. But Hinkle saw a darker side to it.

To truly understand this part of the story, one has to get a fuller picture of just how ill she had become. As with many people who have chronic illnesses, which erupt and then subside, it was not always easy to see how sick Lu Anne was. When not having an acute attack, she could look well, her beauty still shimmering, her mood still upbeat—the very picture of health. But, in fact, she had come close to dying at least three times already. In 1957, in Tampa, an attack of her IBS had caused her so much pain that she'd been hospitalized. Annie recalls that her survival was touch and go for a few days, and that when she was finally released, she was still extremely weak and fearful that she would not recover. That was when she drafted a desperate letter to Neal, printed later in this book, that she may or may not have ever mailed.

Then in 1962, in San Francisco, she had a hysterectomy, which led to the discovery of 20 stones in her gallbladder that were removed a week later. The two back-to-back surgeries led to severe blood clotting. They had to pump three cups of clotted blood out of her femoral artery; her artery was clogged from her leg all the way to her lung. She remained in the hospital for three months, during which time she almost died twice; and at one point, Joe and Annie were summoned to the hospital because she was being given last rites. Lu Anne was put on Coumadin, a powerful blood thinner, which kept her alive but resulted in frequent bleeding under her skin, which would sometimes leave whole patches of her body black for weeks on end.

Her IBS grew worse too, and for the rest of her life she suffered enormous amounts of pain. She began using Miltowns as well as powerful prescription painkillers. As Annie points out, during the sixties a wide variety of opiate drugs became easily available, and Lu Anne did not shy from using anything that helped her. But according to Al, her moving up to morphine and heroin had much more to do with the connections she retained to San Francisco's club scene through her frequent part-time jobs as bartender and waitress. At some point in North Beach, she met a guy known as Peepers,[*] who

---

[*] Not his actual nickname.

was always trying to find people to help him score hard drugs. He would often start by offering friends a taste of whatever he was using, as a way to get them interested in acquiring more. According to Al, Peepers got Lu Anne hooked on heroin; and for several years in the mid-1970s, her life went straight downhill.

After Joe got out of jail, he opened an after-hours music-and-dancing joint in the Tenderloin called the 181 Club, at which famous musicians like Nat King Cole sometimes dropped by after their regular gigs. The club was successful, but Joe was tied up for long hours working there. Annie Ree got pregnant, moved out, and began raising her own baby when she was still quite young. With Lu Anne's husband away most of the time, perhaps it was loneliness that got to her, but she began using morphine and heroin more and more heavily.

According to Hinkle, she used up her husband's merchant marine checks to pay for the drugs; and when she again ran out of money, she borrowed against her house, then had trouble making the new mortgage payments. Al knew she was starting to get in too deep when her phone was disconnected. He paid the bill for her, but he recalls that strange people would answer her door when he came over, some of whom didn't even seem to know Lu Anne, and he sensed that they were all high on drugs. Eventually Lu Anne lost her house. At some point, she moved in with Joe, a few blocks from where she used to live, but her desperation for money increased. Al remembers her frequently coming to see him on the railroad, pleading for small loans of 10 or 20 dollars, which he always gave, and promising that she would go into a Methadone treatment program soon. He was appalled by the degrading lifestyle she'd fallen into, and felt ashamed of his own inability to refuse her money, since he knew he was contributing to her downfall by helping finance her habit.

Al recalls that Annie Ree was really worried about her mom at this time, and of course Al and his wife, Helen, were too. Lu Anne's husband, Bob, was highly disapproving of her drug use, in fact would not tolerate it, and so the two separated for a while. At one point, Al says, Lu Anne actually disappeared for almost six months—though it turned out she had merely gone back to Denver. As sympathetic as Al was, and as pained as he felt to witness Lu Anne's humiliation, he was also puzzled and a bit dismayed that a woman in her forties would allow herself to become hooked on hard drugs. He could see people experimenting in their youth, he says, but he felt that somebody in middle age should know better than to embark on such a dangerous lifestyle. It also didn't accord with the Lu Anne he and his wife thought they knew—the woman who was usually so truthful and outgoing and loving, who didn't seem to have a selfish bone in her body, who loved children and in fact often babysat Neal's kids (without Carolyn's knowledge) when they were young, the woman who would endlessly do kind things for her friends, like passing her own daughter's clothes and toys on to the Hinkles for their daughter, Dawn, who was two years younger than Annie Ree.

The only possible explanation Al could come up with for Lu Anne's big downhill detour late in life was that it was "a middle-age thing." He said she would sometimes wonder aloud, "What's left for me?" But it seems there was more than that going on. All the evidence points to the fact that she had never gotten over her love for Neal Cassady, and that the tragic end of his own life was absolutely devastating for her.

Although she truly loved Bob Skonecki, Lu Anne could never break off her sexual relationship with Neal even after she took vows with her fourth husband. The connection she had with Neal seemed to override everything else she had in her life. Al recalls how happy she was—just bubbling over with laughter and merriment—when Neal drove them over to see Jack at his little cottage in Berkeley in

Bob Skonecki (Lu Anne's fourth husband), Lu Anne, and Annie, age 13, holding Junior, her Maltese terrier, Daly City, 1964. (Photo courtesy of Anne Marie Santos.)

1957. He also recalls how worried she was about Neal the following year, when he was in San Quentin. Deeply mortified to have landed in such a place, Neal did not want to write letters to the majority of his friends while in prison (though he did keep up a faithful correspondence with Carolyn). For the most part, he also did not want to see visitors. Lu Anne had no way of getting word of his condition, and she feared for his life. Finally, arrangements were made with the prison, and Al drove her over to Marin County to see him. She asked Al to leave them alone together during the visiting period. Afterward, he says, she was enormously relieved to have found that Neal had achieved some sort of tranquility in jail, and that he was doing his best to earn an early release. It was clear to Al that she still cared a great deal about Neal, and that Neal's state of mind profoundly affected hers, as if there were some sort of communication wire between their psyches.

Al Hinkle with coworker, Southern Pacific Railroad, July 9, 1954. (Photo courtesy of Al Hinkle.)

Hinkle also recalls how, during the sixties, Lu Anne would meet fairly often with Neal for clandestine sex. Until 1963, of course, he was still married to Carolyn; and from late 1963 on, she was married to Skonecki. But the marital status of neither one proved an obstacle to these rendezvous, the urgency of which both Neal and Lu Anne seemed to feel keenly. Occasionally Hinkle would abet their trysts. By prearrangement, Neal would wait in San Jose on certain days when Al brought her down from San Francisco on the train. There'd be big hugs and kisses as soon as they came together, and then Neal would spirit her off in his car to a motel or somebody's empty bedroom, where they'd share a few hours of bliss in each other's arms. Other times—Al learned from Neal—Lu Anne would simply drive down to San Jose in her car and call Neal to come meet her. Her daughter would be left in the care of Joe or one of the many people who spent time living at their house. As far as Hinkle knew, nobody else in their lives, including Carolyn Cassady and Annie Ree, was aware of these secret love meetings.

When Neal was found dying beside the railroad tracks in San Miguel de Allende in 1968, Annie Ree, barely 17, was having her own difficulties and was not there for Lu Anne, to talk through all the things her mother must have been feeling. Nor could Lu Anne easily have talked with Skonecki about Neal's death, even had Skonecki not been absent so much of the time. Joe stayed with her during some of her worst times. Still, Lu Anne retreated into herself. Never much of a drinker, she got so drunk and disoriented one night that she ended up falling asleep in a stranger's house. Four years after Neal's death, she tried heroin, and found herself compelled to ride the self-destructive train almost to the same place where it had taken Jack and Neal.

But Lu Anne proved herself stronger than they were. Maybe it was her love for her child and grandchild that saved her, but one also feels there was a strength in Lu Anne from the very beginning that always let her land on her feet, always kept her one step ahead of the pack of troubles that dogged her for most of her life. After all, as a willowy teenager only halfway through her high school years, she survived the worst tricks and knockdowns a hardened ex-con like Cassady (for in many respects that's what he was) could toss at her. She also survived a host of physically abusive, sometimes brutal men. Some might think there was a streak of masochism in her that brought her back to men like that time and again—but that would have been a matter for a trained therapist to dissect, and she's gone now and beyond the reach of analysis. I would merely suggest here that there is an alternate explanation—that the lady honestly sought love as her highest goal, that she needed love more than anything, craved it, and was willing to risk anything, even her own well-being, to find it.

In any case, according to Hinkle, at some point around the early 1980s, Lu Anne took herself back to Denver again, determined to get off heroin. Hidden away from everyone except her longtime friend Jimmy Holmes, who was himself dying at that time, she put herself through a rehab program and got clean. And as far as anyone knows, she did not use hard drugs ever again for the rest of her life.

She and Skonecki reconciled, took their savings (for she'd managed to keep a little money from the sale of her house), and bought a trailer up in Sonoma County, an hour or so north of San Francisco. There they seemed like the ideal, loving, and contented retired couple. Lu Anne's kindness and thoughtfulness returned in full force. When Al's wife, Helen, died of cancer in 1994, she called him and comforted him greatly. Al returned the favor by visiting Lu Anne several times after Skonecki died in 1995. Bereft herself, she comforted Al again when his second wife, Maxine, whom he married in 1996, fell victim to Alzheimer's disease only a few years later. She remained in her trailer in Sonoma, where Al would find her ensconced amid hundreds of dolls, with a loyal dog for companionship. Her old girlfriend Lois was now dead, and she had also lost her half brother Lloyd, whom she'd been close to.

But she soon found a new companion. She met Joe Sanchez, a Mexican American man who had dated Lloyd's widow for a while. Originally from Los Angeles but now suffering through the Denver winter, he told her he was broke and had no place to stay, so she invited him to move into her spare bedroom in Sonoma. He lived there happily for several years—not so different from the stray people Annie Ree remembers ending up at their house in Daly City several decades earlier. By this time, Lu Anne had her own social security benefits as well as Skonecki's merchant marine pension, and her financial worries were long gone. Just as she always had, she felt it was her duty to help people who were less fortunate than she.

If she were no longer the overtly joyous, impulsive, hell-for-leather young pinup girl she had once been, she was, according to Al, "not unhappy." She had gained a little weight and appeared slightly "plump," but most people found her still beautiful. Whenever they got together, she would ask Al about Ginsberg and other people they knew from the old days who were still alive, like Hal Chase. But when he left a message on her answering machine about Ginsberg reading at Stanford and offered to drive her there and back, she never responded.

Annie and Lu Anne, Lu Anne's last apartment, Clayton Street, San Francisco, 2008. One of the last known photos of Lu Anne. (Photo courtesy of Anne Marie Santos.)

Until she became very sick with cancer during the last year of her life, Lu Anne would call Al about every three or four months to see how he was doing, but she almost never took calls from him or anyone else. She became famous for using her answering machine to screen all her calls, as if she were now relishing her solitude and reluctant to give it up except when she chose to. Often in her calls to check up on him, she'd promise Al that she would "come down soon to see ya," but she never did.

When they did talk, in person or on the phone, he noticed that she avoided talking about Neal, as if the subject came with a pain she didn't want to revive. Likewise, she avoided any specific references to the Beat world, and would brush Al off quickly whenever he suggested she should visit or speak at the new Beat Museum in San Francisco. If he'd ask her questions about their time in New York, she'd always answer him, and even talk readily about it, but she would never bring up the subject herself.

Once, he asked her who the musicians were that they had heard up in Harlem with Jack and Neal. He was astonished when she named every person in that band—she recalled the trumpeter, drummer, clarinetist, every instrument and every player there.

"Her memory was still perfect," he said.

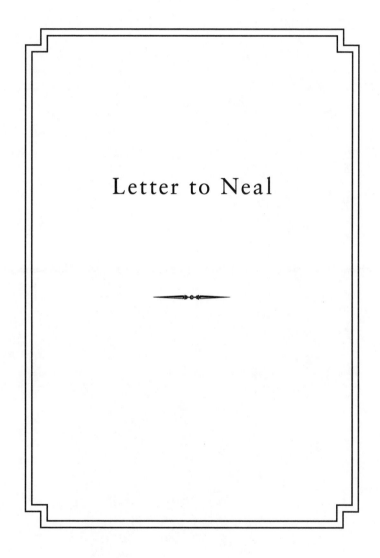

Letter to Neal

A nne Santos found this handwritten, unsent letter among her mother's papers in her San Francisco apartment after her death. It is clearly written to Neal Cassady. Anne believes it was written in Tampa, Florida, in 1957, just after her mom got out of the hospital following a serious illness, during which Lu Anne may have had to confront her possible death. The handwriting, in light-blue pen, has faded over the years, and her spelling and punctuation are nonstandard, so deciphering the letter was no easy task. In one place, where I was not certain of the reading, I marked the doubtful word with a question mark.—G.N.

Lu Anne's letter to Neal from Tampa, Florida, 1957, page 1. (Ccourtesy of Anne Marie Santos.)

Neal,

I've suddenly realized at this late date that you're my what? I don't know what really, all I know is that as I'm sitting here in Tampa I can't stand the thought of not knowing you. I can't put down what I'm feeling & yet I'm trying. I wonder can I put down the emotion within me, even when I'm with another, someday, someway, I'm listening to Frank Sinatra. Oh Neal I love you. Have you ever just sat & wrote what you felt. I feel you as much now as when I was sixteen. I don't know if you're a hangover or am I mad. I've made so many moves, but not until this last year have I realized why. Neal please. I started to say please help me & I don't really know if it was pride or once again I'm stumped. I'm sitting here with my head in my hand trying to say the right thing. What is the right thing. Even when I say I love you I cringe. You've dominated most of my life, & if I could feel your arms around me I could go on forever. Is that theatrical? I'm just talking baby. Just anything to ease some of this torment. Somehow you've become like some irritation on the skin and keep getting bigger and bigger & even when you squeeze it, no it's not gone, just a permanent scar (forever). Is that the way it is. I hate to think I'm a martyr [?], and yet do I. I don't really know & once again I'm back to saying please help me not in the usual sense, but I started to say because we're friends. I love you or whatever it is Neal & can't get over it. You have to teach me, tell me know me & mostly I want you to love me with your lips, your eyes, your hands & as always just to have you walk to me, you make love to me. I'm afraid Neal that you left me as a child & will once again find me the same, I take that back. I just got mad at myself for thinking that, you won't find me a child, maybe in ways, but talk to me & love me & you'll find I'm a woman, but more than that, you'll find I'm a woman you've molded without ever being near. I know how you think, but regardless you motivated more things in my life than anyone living.

[The letter breaks off, unsigned.]

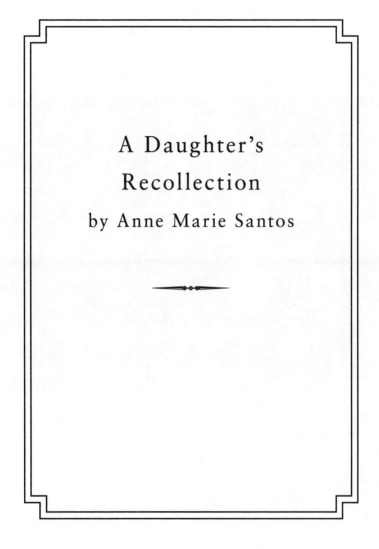

A Daughter's Recollection

by Anne Marie Santos

Lu Anne presenting trophy to the winner of the Midget Auto Races, Denver, 1944 or 1945. (Photo courtesy of Anne Marie Santos.)

My Mother was Lu Anne, the model for "Marylou" in *On the Road*. She is known to most of the literary world as Lu Anne Henderson, although she was born Cora Lu Anne Bullard.

She also had the surnames Cassady, Murphy, Catechi, and Skonecki. Each one of these names represents a husband: Neal Cassady, Ray Murphy, Sam Catechi, and Bob Skonecki. But each also represents a different time in her life. Even more than that, they really were clear and separate lives—each having the joys and sorrows of love found and lost. Mother always spoke with love and kindness of all of these men with whom she shared her life, though in later years she would reflect on the hardships she endured while living with some of them. All of these husbands—including eventually even Ray Murphy, from whom she'd initially had to hide for a couple of years after their divorce—remained loving toward her, just as almost all the people she met throughout her life remained her friends. She was one of those people who drew others in to want to know her. She invited you in by her smile and sparkling eyes. Her

Lu Anne, age 16, Peetz, Colorado. (Photo courtesy of Anne Marie Santos.)

gentle, warm greeting, "Hi honey," got them at the first hello. Being pretty, smart, humble, caring, and a good listener didn't hurt either. I always describe her as a cross between Auntie Mame and Holly Golightly.

My friends were always envious of her; they always said that I was the only one with a "fun mother." Since I was an only child, she made sure I always had friends around. When I was little and she worked at San Francisco Airport as a cocktail waitress, she would rent a motel room for the day at Casa Mateo, which was close by, and we would swim all day until she got ready for work. Or she would take a carload of her friends and us kids to Marin Town and Country Club for barbecue and swimming. In the summer she would rent a cabin at Rio Nido on the Russian River, and over the summer people took turns staying with us. One summer she surprised us with tickets to see the Beatles at the Cow Palace. She had her friend Joe come and pick us up in Rio Nido and deliver us back after the show. She loved playing board games and cards or just playing records and singing and dancing around the house. One of the highlights for my two best friends, Tina and Sharon, was to put on shows with me for my mother and her friends. She would let us get in her closet and wear all her beautiful dresses, high heels, furs, and jewelry—nothing was off-limits.

We went out to dinner all the time and saw floor shows at places like Bimbo's 365 Club, Sinaloa Mexican restaurant, and the Forbidden City in Chinatown. She always got the best seats, and my friends and I would usually be asked on stage because she almost always knew someone who worked there. She even took Sharon to Las Vegas one time by herself because I had been there with my mother the year before and didn't want to go again. They saw *Flower Drum Song*, and through my mother Sharon met Joey Bishop. Kids felt they could confide in her when they needed an adult to really listen to them. All my friends remained close with her.

Though we were surrounded by many friends who loved us, when I was very young I would always wonder why we seemed to have no family. She would tell me that we actually had a very large family back in Colorado and that we would go visit sometime. But we never did. Sometimes she told me about how her great-grandparents and grandparents had homesteaded large tracts of land around Peetz, Colorado, and that those ranches were still thriving. I knew that my grandparents were in England, because "Pappy," as I called my grandfather, was in the Air Force. When Pappy and his wife, Thelma, came back to the United States, he was stationed in Florida. They had been there when I was born; then he was stationed overseas for a few years. They would send gifts at the holidays, which are some of my earliest recollections of them: Christmas stockings with nuts and oranges, and a tea set that I still have. My mother's half brothers moved to Los Angeles when I was about five years old, and soon after that we did make a trip there so that I could meet my family for the first time.

Flying to Los Angeles was my first big trip. We got to the airport late, because Mother was never one to watch a clock. The gate was closed and the stairs were pulled back from the plane. But since she worked at the airport lounge, she knew some of the ground crews there. As the plane was pulling away, she managed to talk one of the airport workers into stopping the plane. "Oh, honey, I really need to get to L.A.," etc, etc, she rattled on, and sure enough the plane stops, turns back, the stairs are rolled back out, and up we go. In the same way, she could talk her way into clubs where the act was sold out and there were no seats left. She could talk anybody into just about anything.

As a child, I tended to be embarrassed over everything she did to call attention to herself, but when Mother rolled into the plane that day, laughing and smiling, all I could hear were people whispering, "Is she a movie star?" or, "Is that Doris Day?" Later in life, with her hair short and bleached, she actually did look a lot like Doris Day, or maybe Kim Novak. Anyway, we made our flight and spent the weekend with family. As a surprise, she took me and her nieces and nephew to Disneyland, which had just been opened. So for me it was a magical weekend. Seeing these cousins was a rare treat, but I felt very close to them. Besides her two brothers, Lloyd and Lowell, Mother had eleven aunts and uncles and 41 first cousins, and she said that drama followed wherever her family went. That, she explained, was why we were better off living in California. The suggestion was that she was trying to avoid drama, or maybe she'd just had too much of it in her life already. Still, she would do anything for family members when they asked, and they were always asking.

I knew nothing of the Bullard side of the family—her father's side. She loved her father very deeply, but had a guilt about their relationship that burdened her terribly. It all stemmed from her childhood. When she was only four years old, she left the only home she had known, in Peetz, Colorado, up on those mountain ranches, and moved to Los Angeles to live with her father and his new wife and two daughters.

Mother was born March 1, 1930, during the Depression years, and life was extremely difficult in the farming communities everywhere. Her parents' marriage did not survive the economic stresses, and her father, James Astor Bullard, moved to Los Angeles and found work as a private security guard and later as a member of the Compton police force. Los Angeles was growing, and he had job security as well as the opportunity to get ahead. He persuaded her mother, Thelma Stone, that he could provide better for Lu Anne at that time. "Gramps" (which is what we all call my grandmother) had two older sons from a previous marriage, who were old enough

Lu Anne, less than a year old, Peetz, Colorado. (Photo courtesy of Anne Marie Santos.)

Lu Anne, age 6, and her mother, Thelma Stone Henderson, Union Station, Denver. At age 4, Lu Anne was sent to live with her father in Los Angeles. She traveled by herself once a year to visit her mother. (Photo courtesy of Anne Marie Santos.)

to work and help on the Stone family farm, so she agreed that it would be for the best to send Lu Anne to Los Angeles for a while. That "while" ended up being eight years.

Mother lived in Compton and Venice during her school years and recalled that they were very lonely. She was friendly with her two stepsisters and said she adored the older one, Marion, but was always in competition with the younger one, "Baby," over her father's affection. My granddad, the policeman, was very strict, and life with him was very rigid. Early on, he did have a job working for Jack Benny, who was a radio and movie star before his hit television show. She recalled times when she would visit Benny's house for a birthday party, and how she received lovely gifts such as a porcelain doll set of the Dionne quintuplets. For fun, Mother used to play at being in radio shows. Then Granddad became a policeman, and his attitude seemed to become a lot more serious, as he emphasized to Lu Anne that she must follow rules without question. She was a good student and from all accounts very sweet and warm—an all-around good girl. But she never felt truly at home in Los Angeles. When she would tell me these stories of waiting for her mother and brothers to come rescue her and take her back to her real home, I always pictured her as poor little Cinderella.

The day finally arrived when her mother came to visit, when Lu Anne was about 12. At the end of her mother's stay, her father took my mom aside and told her that her mother wanted to take her back to Denver.

Whenever my mother told this story, this is the place where she would break down. My mother said she did not give it a second thought—she packed in five minutes and was so, so, so happy to leave. She kissed her dad goodbye and did not look back. She would always say, "All those years he raised me, loved me, and I did not even consider staying with him."

To make matters worse, when she started school in Denver that year, 1942, she changed her last name to Henderson so it would match her mother's, who had married Stephen Henderson, an Air Force photographer. She just wanted to fit in at school with the same name as her family, so no one would know she was from a broken home. When her father found out what she had done, he wrote her a hurtful letter, accusing her of betraying him. Furious, he said he felt his name was "no longer good enough" for her. After that, they did not communicate for years. Not until almost a decade later, after I was born, did she finally visit with him. At that time, she was introduced to her half brother Dan, who was only a year older that me. The problems between them must have been more than they were willing to forgive, because I never knew my Granddad Bullard or his

Lu Anne with her father, James Bullard, Los Angeles, 1938. (Photo courtesy of Anne Marie Santos.)

family until many years later when Dan and I connected through a genealogy site. Mother believed her dad was a brokenhearted man for many years after she left him, and she carried that guilt for life.

Even though she used the name Henderson, her relationship with her stepfather, Steve, was rocky. The life in Denver was quite a bit different than her life in Los Angeles had been. She said she was shocked to see her mother drink and smoke, which her father would never have allowed with the Bullard women. Her mother owned Thelma's Crystal Bar. She recalled quarrels between her mother and Steve, on nights when she would come back late from the bar, that often left Thelma with black eyes. She had never seen a man hit or abuse a woman before, and so she became very angry and lashed out at Steve verbally as well as physically, especially once she became a teenager. Though Steve and Gramps remained married the rest of their lives, Lu Anne's rift with Steve was never repaired; but they did eventually learn to tolerate each other for Gramps's sake.

There were many instances of abuse in Lu Anne's subsequent marriages. Mother never indicated to me that her relationship with Neal was violent, but there is the well-documented punch at her head which landed on the wall instead, and left his hand somewhat handicapped. The marriage to my father, Ray Murphy, lasted less than two years due to alcoholism and the frequent beatings he gave her. After the annulment with Neal, Mother married Murphy, my father, in a civil ceremony on April 14, 1949, in Denver. He arrived at the wedding drunk, meeting Gramps and Steve for the first time at the ceremony. Mother was extremely embarrassed but went through with the wedding anyway, though she should have been warned of things to come. During the next year, while she was pregnant with me, she went to catechism every day at St. Ignatius Church in San Francisco, which was right across the street from our house on Stanyan. She converted to Catholicism for her Irish Catholic husband so that they could marry again in church before I was born. Their "official" Catholic wedding took place at St. Agnes Church on November 15, 1950. I was born December 18, 1950.

My father was a merchant marine when they met, but got into sales that first year. She said all went well for a while; but when this Irishman drank, his temper flared and even slight disagreements could escalate into violence. After he repeatedly put her in the hospital with a broken nose and bruises, she wanted out. The final straw was him holding me out an open window as a threat to try to make her stay.

Mother had originally converted to Catholicism to satisfy her husband, without much belief in it. The only churches she remembered from Colorado were the revival-meeting tents, where the preacher would terrify everyone with fire-and-brimstone sermons, which put her off from religion for quite a long time. But increasingly she went to Catholic church now for comfort, and her belief in the religion grew. The church became her safety net, and she spoke to her priest about Ray. Though he dutifully advised her on marriage laws—which demanded, in essence, that a wife stick with her husband through thick and thin, beatings or no beatings—he also, secretly, gave her enough money to escape by bus to friends in Clear Lake, California. She told me she left with only my clothes and a bag of oranges for us to eat. That summer, a single mother for the first time, she found a job waiting tables. She eventually came back to San Francisco and filed for divorce. I never met my father until I was 14 years old, and then there was no further contact with me for several years, though he did send cards to us once in a while. In later years, he and my mother would sometimes visit each other, and—with the old wounds finally healed—they seemed concerned about each other's lives.

For the next few years, she and I lived alone in the city. She worked at various clubs in North Beach as a cocktail waitress and eventually met and married Sam Catechi, who owned the Little Bohemia nightclub. I was three years old when they married. The following year, they bought a house in Daly City, which is the house I grew up in. Mother kept it until about 1978. I really don't know the reasons this marriage failed, though they stayed close friends for life, and I always called him Daddy. It was during this time that Mother started having serious medical problems.

She had always been bothered with stomach issues—a cluster of symptoms that are known collectively as irritable bowel syndrome. She had had a tube pregnancy while married to Sam and suffered greatly with gynecological issues after that. It was in 1957 that she became so ill we rented out our house and moved to Florida to stay with Gramps and Pappy (Steve). She was hospitalized many times during that year and, the last time, almost didn't make it home. Upon her release, she wrote the letter to Neal telling him how important his love had been to her. Eventually she felt better and wanted to get back to San Francisco. She flew back to California ahead of me and got the house ready for us, and then I joined her, flying alone for the first time at eight years old. She and Sam picked me up at the airport with a new puppy named Coco for me.

Our home in Daly City was not the typical suburban house. At one point, we had chocolate-brown walls covered with primitive African oil paintings. Over the fireplace was a picture of two natives, a man and a woman, that scared me every time I looked at it. Their eyes always seemed to be watching me. Mother was not your typical PTA mom. Since she normally worked nights, she would sleep till at least noon most days. It would not be unusual for me to wake in the morning for school to a living room thick with cigarette smoke, full of people I'd never met before listening to jazz, or maybe having a deep philosophical discussion that involved Jack Kerouac, though at that time I did not know who he was.

On weekends, you could find anyone from the chief of police to female impersonators from Finocchio's hanging about, having drinks or sipping coffee together. People from all walks of life—from writers to Teamsters to homeless folk—all found their way to my mother's door. We always joked that if there was a nut within 10 miles they could find her. She took in many people over the years that needed care. A pregnant woman who worked for her close friend Joe needed to get away from her abusive husband. Mother took her in for about six months, and she became the little girl's godmother. She had at least 10 godchildren throughout her life. Once a neighbor sold her house and moved away, but left her tenant in the basement. The tenant, a woman, had emphysema and was an ex-con. Mother put her in our extra bedroom, and she lived there for the next five years.

Life with my mother was never dull, though I often found myself disapproving of her behavior. I was always the conservative one, and she was the free spirit. In many ways, I was the mother and she the child. A few years back, she visited me in Virginia, and we drove over to the Edgar Cayce Institute in Virginia Beach. We had read his book *The Sleeping Prophet* when I was quite young, and I have since learned that Neal and Carolyn Cassady were big followers of his. We went to a lecture and past-lives reading. According to the reader, my mother and I actually did have our roles reversed in one of our previous lives. We are supposedly destined to go through our many lives as best friends, mother, and daughter in many different combinations.

There was one area, though, in which I learned some very important lessons from her. Lu Anne had a profound understanding—an almost inborn understanding—of how wrong racism was. Her experience with it began in California at the start of World War II. In Los Angeles, she had Japanese schoolmates, one of whom became a very close friend of hers. After Pearl Harbor, this girl, along with all the other Japanese in the area, were hauled off to internment camps. Many of them lost their homes and everything they had. Only 12 years old, Lu Anne was crushed by the loss of her friend, and angry at what seemed to her such an obvious injustice. Then, when she returned to Denver, a new face of racism showed itself in the prejudice against Mexicans. My mother always loved to dance, and she told me how the best-looking boys, as well as the best dancers, were usually Mexican. When she mentioned her interest in certain Mexican boys, however, Thelma was aghast. She told Lu Anne, "You do not socialize with Mexicans. You do not go out on a date with them. It's simply not done. A nice white girl like you does not date a Mexican." My mother just did not understand. She would always ask, "What's the problem?" and nobody gave her any answer that made sense to her.

As she began to strike out on her own in Denver—in her years of teenage rebellion—she would go to the all-black jazz clubs in Five Points, and she began to be exposed not only to different races, but to people with a variety of different lifestyles. She was always very accepting and very friendly to everyone, and she gave everyone the opportunity to be themselves. In later years, she made a point of inviting people of all races, nationalities, and economic levels into her home. When she moved to Florida in 1957—when it was still the Deep South—she encountered the real, hard-core racism against blacks. She got a job at Vic Tanny's fitness club, which had both black and white employees. But the employees were kept completely segregated. There was no intermingling in the lunch area. My mother had become friendly with several of the black employees, and one day she brought her lunch over and sat down with some of them. As she prepared to eat her lunch, the boss walked over and told her it was not acceptable for her to eat lunch, or even to sit down, in the "colored section." My mother refused to move; and after that, she ate lunch in the designated black area every day. For some reason, they didn't fire her.

When I was growing up, she would tell me, very pointedly, that I should never judge anyone by their race, religion, color, or their status in life—that I should accept everyone as an equal, even if they were homeless. And I saw her practice what she preached. She always befriended people from all walks of life.

And then there were the things we did together that weren't about life lessons or had anything to do with other people—they were just wonderful mother-daughter times we had together. There are so many good times I had with her that had nothing to do with her Beat life, which so many people now want to hear about. For one thing, she loved to cook—maybe because early on she didn't know how, and she had had to teach herself. So it became a hobby and also a way for her to relax, to experiment and be creative. She would never go by recipes. She would start cooking at seven or eight o'clock at night; and by the time she got done, we'd have a six-course meal waiting for us—it might be roast beef, mashed potatoes, salad, all the trimmings—at eleven o'clock at night! Sometimes it would be pasta or a fancy stew. By the time it was ready, if it was a school night, I'd grab a few mouthfuls and then have to go to bed. And I'd end up eating roast beef with mashed potatoes and gravy for breakfast. Lu Anne just loved cooking those big dinners, and she also loved inviting people over for big dinner parties. She was known as a very, very good cook.

The love of fine clothing was another thing she shared with me. She'd always loved fine clothing. When she was pregnant with me, one of her jobs was modeling at one of the bigger department stores downtown—it might have been Emporium Capwell. In those days, the stores had ladies who would walk the runways to show their clothing lines. Lu Anne did this till she was eight months pregnant, because she was so thin—incredibly, nobody noticed that she was carrying me! She was five foot seven and a half inches tall, and with heels she was easily five foot nine, and she weighed only 112 pounds. She could wear clothes beautifully; she had that long, lean, elegant look. She had a closet full of Lilli Ann suits—she knew all the names of the lines. She'd take me to a famous women's tailor in San Francisco—I think her name was Olga Galgano—and have outfits tailormade for both of us. Lu Anne had fur stoles, a hundred pairs of shoes—most of them high heels—and purses that matched every outfit. She had charge accounts at all the good stores. One of her favorites was I. Magnin, but we'd go to all of them, including City of Paris. She kept all her clothes for decades, took immaculate care of them—until a big fire in our house in 1960 destroyed just about everything we had.

There was one other benefit of having Lu Anne as a mom. She knew all the cops in San Francisco. I remember once when I was about 16, getting pulled over in a car full of kids, and the cops started to take our names. When they got to me, and I said, "Anne Catechi," the cop lifted an eyebrow and asked, "Are you Lu Anne's daughter?" When I said yes, he let us go!

Eventually, of course, the Beat world intruded into our cozy domesticity—as it was bound to do. I think my mother kept it away from our household as long as she could partly because of her not wanting any more drama in her life, and her feeling that we already had enough drama with Joe, his clubs, and all the characters who kept wandering through our home—not to mention her frequent medical emergencies and everything else. She knew that the Beats were high drama, and she didn't want to be drawn back into it, didn't want it to come into our everyday life. It was certainly not her best day when Neal Cassady showed up at our house.

It was 1966, and I was already enjoying the Bay Area counterculture. Despite my mother's warnings to "stay away from Bill Graham and that crowd he hangs around with," I'd already been to the Fillmore Auditorium many times—to see Janis Joplin and Big Brother, Steppenwolf, the Grateful Dead, and so many other great countercultural bands. Of course, my mother was right—people were doing every kind of drug that you could imagine at those concerts. I wasn't doing the drugs, but I liked the music. We lived in Daly City, but I went to all the free concerts in Golden Gate Park, and to the Haight-Ashbury to buy earrings and peasant skirts. I grew up in the era of the hippies, so I must admit that Beats, beatniks, and the Beat Generation were as far from my world as the flappers of the 1920s.

Lu Anne, Sonoma, between 2000 and 2003. (Photo courtesy of Anne Marie Santos.)

I was 16 years old when I met Neal Cassady, and I was absolutely baffled when he showed up at our house. My boyfriend Gene and I were home one afternoon when I opened the door to a man asking for my mother. Nothing special struck me about him, except he looked a little wild-eyed, like he was on speed. It was his introduction that left a lasting impression on me, and not in a positive way. He said, "I'm Neal, and I was your mother's first husband. And you are not nearly as pretty as Al Hinkle said you are." I don't even remember what was said after that! You don't tell a 16-year-old girl she's not pretty. The husband part was just an afterthought. He let me know that he and his friends needed a place to sleep, but I wasn't about to ask them in. Of course, by the time my mother arrived home, I was pacing. The DayGlo-painted bus "Furthur" was still parked in front of our house.

"Who is this crazy person?" I demanded. After my mom dealt with Neal and his friends, she came back in and said, "Yes, I did get married when I was quite young in Denver, and then we divorced and I came to California. That's when I met your dad and married him." Since Lu Anne's marriage to my dad had only lasted a year, I did not know my biological father either—so now there were two previous husbands I was in the dark about. It was clear my mom was uneasy about the visit and didn't want to tell me any more than she had to about Neal, so I didn't ask her any more questions. I was used to her keeping parts of her life off-limits to me, and I didn't want to make her uncomfortable by prying into those areas. Plus I was always much more interested in her stories from the time we called "the Jack Benny years," when her father worked for United Artists Studios and was the bodyguard for Mr. Benny, in the 1930s.

It turned out—I later learned—that the bus had been filled with Pranksters and members of the Grateful Dead, who'd been hoping to come in our house to crash for a while. If I had known that, being a big fan of the Dead, I would probably have invited them in with open arms.

It's funny that I could grow up and be so totally unaware of such an attachment as my mom's love for Neal. I was aware, even despite the long distance, of her half brothers and other people in her life—people who'd been significant in Denver, for instance. But I have no recollection of Neal ever being around until that day when he showed up in the painted bus. My mother did not include him, or invite him, into any part of our life. She still kept that relationship totally separate. To think that there was someone my mother had been so close to—and this life she had been so much wrapped up in—and yet I was totally unaware of it, seems strange. My mother usually was open, but she kept that part, the Beat part, totally compartmentalized, so that it was not part of my world at all. I think she just put that part of her life away. If Neal would reach out, she'd be there for him, but she didn't want that to be her life, her reality, now.

Later on, I actually wondered why she didn't bring him over and say, "Oh, hey, this is Neal," instead of keeping him so sequestered from me. It also amazed me that he actually abided by that. He seemed like the type who would selfishly drop in when he felt like it, but for most of those years he'd always go through Al Hinkle when he needed to see her, and Al would come and pick her up. When he did finally drop in with the bus and the Grateful Dead, in 1966 or 1967, it was close to the end of his life. Maybe he didn't care anymore.

It took my mother years to finally open up to me, and to start telling me her Beat stories. She always made it seem as if the Beats were not a big deal. It was not until *Heart Beat* was being filmed in 1978, and people started showing up wanting to interview her, that I began to get a little hint that Lu Anne had led some sort of life different than the one I'd known. But the only thing I heard at that point was that a friend of my mother's had been a writer and had written a book—that it was about some people in New York that people were now interested in. My mother made it seem like the main interest in the movie was that these famous actors like Sissy Spacek and Nick Nolte were in it. She still didn't talk to me about the Beat Generation or beatniks. I remember that I did sense some rivalry she had with Carolyn Cassady, because when Al would drive her to the set in San Francisco, she always made sure she looked her best. Sometimes she would even borrow my clothes to look more modern, to look younger, knowing people would be comparing her to Carolyn. I knew that my mother's first husband was one of the people they were making the movie about, but that was all.

When my mother did finally start to tell me her Beat stories, they were mostly the famous ones that I'd already heard—about her running off to Nebraska with Neal when she was 16, stealing her aunt's money, going to New York and meeting Jack Kerouac, and so forth. But there was one funny story I remember, about when Neal had taken her up to his cabin up in the mountains, and they were having a big drunken party with some of his friends, using pot too, and there were a lot of underage girls present. Somebody called the cops, and they all got arrested and taken to the jail in Golden, Colorado. At first, my mother refused to give the cops her name, so they locked her up with a woman who had murdered her baby. This woman was really tough; she claimed she knew gangsters from Chicago, and she told my mom they could break out of jail together. My mother played along with her. The woman asked Lu Anne if she could get a car. My mother said, "No problem." Then the woman asked her, "Can you get any guns?" My mom answered, "Guns? Got 'em!" Of course, eventually Lu Anne had to give her name, and they released her to her family. But when she told Neal the story, he laughed, and whenever he wanted to tease her, he'd look at her and say, "Guns? Got 'em!" and they'd both crack up.

The thing was, my mother really seemed to have a lot of scorn for the people who wanted to learn about the Beats. In the early '70s, and even into the '80s, Lu Anne would kind of laugh about the way the Beat fans idolized them, how these people would think all their cross-country rides were the best of times. "We were just kids, just surviving," my mother told me. "If we needed to go somewhere, we'd hop into a car and drive. Maybe the car didn't belong to Neal, since if he needed to get somewhere he'd grab any car he could find. If you were freezing to death and you needed a coat, you just took it, or if you needed food and you were broke, you'd get up from a restaurant without paying. We were surviving—it wasn't a joyride by any stretch of the imagination." Lu Anne would scoff at people who would say, "Oh, you people must have had the time of your life—you were so freewheeling!"

But she laughed the most at the people who wanted to recreate what they'd done. In the 1970s, some woman came to see her and told her, "I took the same trips you took—I followed your footsteps across the country." My mother said to me, "Who would want to recreate freezing to death and starving to death? We went for a purpose. Neal wanted to become a writer. Like everybody else does when they're eighteen or twenty, you go somewhere, you might starve for a while, but you're trying to build your life and your dream."

When my mom finally told me these stories, she stressed to me that they had just been trying to live their lives; they weren't thinking they were creating this generation that people were going to follow. And of course there was a slow evolution in her own understanding of it as well. Jack's novel was a big deal when it came out in 1957; but then by the late 1960s, most of his books were out of print. No one was coming to see her then, no one was looking her up to ask her questions; and it wasn't till the late 1970s, when people started writing books about them and Carolyn's movie got made, that my mother began to realize that this is bigger than just about me, just my story, it's something that a lot of people in the world want to know about. Earlier, in the '50s and '60s, she'd never dreamed that people were going to seek her out, that they would want to find out all about her life and the lives of her friends.

In the last few years, my mother became interested in the fact that Francis Ford Coppola, and then Walter Salles, was going to make a movie of *On the Road*, and her story was actually going to be told in a bigger and hopefully better way than it had been in *Heart Beat*. She kept waiting for them to get started with the filming, but it didn't happen till after she died. I felt sad about that, that she didn't live to see the movie come out. But I was glad when Walter Salles asked me to come up to Montreal to talk to the actors, especially Kristen Stewart, who was going to play my mom. It gave me a chance to try to tell the story she would have told them, had she lived.

When I went to Montreal, I was a little concerned about the fact that Kristen didn't seem the right type to play my mother. I had to keep forcing myself to remember that she was representing a fictional character in a book, that this was not actually a biography of my mother. I didn't think that Kristen could actually try to be my mother, because she's totally opposite of my mother in so many ways. Kristen is small, petite, with an almost brooding type of personality, where my mother was bubbly, smiley, full of sunshine. My mother was gentle; Kristen swears quite a bit, she's foul-mouthed and comes on tough. But once I met her, she was very curious about what it was like to grow up with my mother, what kind of experience I had as a child with a mother who had been through this whole adventure. Kristen just wanted to know about my whole experience as a child.

I found that Kristen is very, very committed to the part, that she wants to represent my mother in her own right, not as "a shadow

Lu Anne's best friend, Lois, and Lu Anne wearing her swing coat, Market Street, San Francisco, 1948. (Photo courtesy of Anne Marie Santos.)

Anne Marie Santos and Sam Riley on the set of On the Road, *San Francisco, December 2010. Anne Marie, Lu Anne's daughter, worked as a body double for Kristen Stewart. (Photo by Gerald Nicosia.)*

to the boys," as she put it. She was very protective of my mother, and very defensive about what Carolyn Cassady had written about her. Kristen felt that Carolyn was trying to make my mother look bad, that she treated my mother as if she was cheap and low-class. Carolyn had written the story as if she was the socialite, and as if my mother was just this young girl who was easy, who was brought along just as a sex object for these guys. Kristen felt that Carolyn had not portrayed my mother in a very good light, that she'd made her seem like just this young kid Neal happened to marry before he knew any better. She told me straight off that that was *not* how she wanted to play the role of Lu Anne.

Kristen told me that some agent didn't just present her with the part. She said she had read *On the Road* early on in her life, when she was maybe 13 or 14. She told me, "I have the original book where I highlighted the parts of Marylou." She was already interested in the story when she just started her teens! I thought that was amazing, because I didn't even read *On the Road* till I was 40. I also thought it was interesting that she'd gotten so attached to the book, because *On the Road* is usually considered a book that guys are into. "My curiosity about Lu Anne didn't just come up when Walter Salles asked me to read for the part," she said. She explained that what fascinated her about Lu Anne—"Marylou"—was that she was a young, strong woman, independent and adventurous, holding her own with the boys—that was how Kristen described her. She told me, "The three of them are all equal in this trip, in this relationship. Lu Anne has as much influence and responsibility for what's happening as they do. It's not just the boys telling her what to do, dragging her along. She's not just some dumb airhead."

I learned that Kristen had started acting professionally very young, when she was nine or ten years old. By the time she was in her early teens, she was already an independent actress—and she was looking for role models who could show her the way. She was looking for someone "who had already done it"—by which she meant a young woman who'd also struck out on her own at a very young age. When the part of Marylou came up, she was just so excited to be able to try out for it. She wanted to portray Marylou as a real person. For her, it's not a fictional character, and that's what made the difference in her acting in this part. Sure, they're making a movie of a book, but Kristen is not just playing Marylou. She's playing Lu Anne.

Walter Salles was pushing all the actors in the direction of doing *On the Road* as the story of real people, but Kristen had the same intention even before she met with Walter. Kristen told me that when she listened to the tapes of Lu Anne telling her story, that was the moment when Marylou became Lu Anne for her. She could then see her, hear her, as the very young woman she had been when Neal and Jack first knew her.

Kristen and I spent the day alone out on the porch of that loft in Montreal, and she was in tears some of the time, when I was talking about my mother and some of the hurts she had been through—when I was telling her about my mother's illnesses and her divorces. Kristen is a very feeling young woman. She's only a girl of 20 years, but when she's researching a part, she goes all the way into it. I just remember when I told her the story about my mother and the poster of Neal, Kristen was tremendously moved. Some guy had obtained this huge poster of Neal, and he was taking it all over the country—maybe to other countries too—and getting anyone connected with the Beats to sign it. He brought the poster to my mother for her to sign. Lu Anne looked at it, it was almost completely filled up with signatures, but there was still an open space around Neal's heart. So she signed it there, and wrote, "You are my heart. I love you forever, Lu Anne." That story made Kristen cry.

What was funny was that Kristen was actually worried about me, how I would react to the movie. She acted as if she were trying to protect me. "Some of the scenes are pretty rough now," she said. "Don't be shocked when you see them. You know the story, but the way we're doing it is pretty graphic and pretty rough." I just smiled. It was very cute, very sweet, but I'm not worried about the graphic scenes. What's important to me is that Kristen really seems to feel what my mother went through.

I saw her again in Baton Rouge a couple of months later. She was already done filming her parts in *On the Road*, and had moved on to start filming the next *Twilight* episode. She cooked dinner for me and my husband, Reuben, and I learned that Kristen likes to cook, and uses cooking to relax, just like my mother did. She told me she hoped to see me at the wrap party for the film in San Francisco in

December [2010], and that was one of the reasons I came out to California then. It turned out that Kristen was still tied up with her latest film and couldn't make it, but I got an even more memorable experience.

The day after I arrived in San Francisco, I got a call from Walter Salles's assistant, Alex Killian. She asked me, "Were your ears burning last night? We were talking about you, and Walter had this great idea that it would be so exciting if you could play your mother in the movie." It was the next-to-last day of filming, and they were shooting the scene where Neal, Jack, and Lu Anne have just arrived in San Francisco after their cross-country drive from New Orleans. Neal is racing them around the hills in his Hudson, getting ready to drop them off in front of some hotel so he can go back to Carolyn. Since Kristen was no longer available, they needed a body double to play her in the car, sitting between Jack and Neal. They'd chosen me to be the body double for my mom.

The next day, they took me to the makeup trailer, and got me all fixed up to look like Marylou (Lu Anne). I got to wear the same coat that Kristen had worn—a swing coat with one button, that had been designed to look like one that my mom had actually worn in some photographs from the '40s—and the same "dirty blonde" wig that Kristen had worn too. "Are you sure that sixty can play sixteen?" I asked them, but Alex assured me that no one would really get a good look at me. She said she had played Kristen's body double on several occasions, and there was even some guy on the set who claimed *he* had played her body double once or twice when no one else was available.

So there I was, dressed up like my mom 60 years ago, meeting Garrett Hedlund and Sam Riley, who were dressed up like Neal and Jack 60 years ago. The thing was, everyone was so excited to have me there. I talked to Rebecca Yeldham, one of the producers who

Garrett Hedlund (Neal Cassady), Gerald Nicosia, Sam Riley (Jack Kerouac), Kristen Stewart (Lu Anne Henderson), on the porch at "Beat Boot Camp." (Photo courtesy of Gerald Nicosia.)

had followed the filming from state to state and country to country. They'd been on the road themselves for almost five months. Rebecca told me, "It's been such a long shoot, everybody's so tired. This is just what we need to put some fun and excitement back into the movie. It brings us full circle to where we started." Everybody on the set was so up to have me there; they were all laughing and having so much fun with the idea that I was playing Kristen playing my mother.

We were supposed to zoom up Filbert Street in the Hudson and round the corner almost on two wheels onto Leavenworth, then shoot on up the hill and out of view. The gag was that as we were coming up the hill on Filbert, this extra, a young woman in a 1940s outfit, had to hurry across the street to get out of our way. But during the first few takes, the Hudson didn't get close enough to her to satisfy Walter, so we had to keep redoing it.

After the third take, Sam Riley, who was playing Jack, looked at me and said, "I want you to remember this moment. Every time you see this scene in the movie, you must remember the three of us sharing this moment together. You must remember that we shared our own on-the-road moment, and when I see this scene I'll think of our moment together too. I'll never forget this scene." Sam was unbelievably sweet.

Jack was supposed to be carrying a book with him across the country. Just before we'd start up the hill, Sam would put the book up on the dash; and then when Garrett would go squealing around the corner, the book would slide off. It became a little game with Sam that he'd always try to catch the book as it came hurtling toward him. Everything needed to be exactly the same in each take. But when we paused at the bottom of the hill between takes, the guys would throw open the car doors and roll down the windows, and crew members would come up and give us something to drink or just talk to us. During all the previous takes, all four windows had been rolled up; but on one of the last takes, as we started up the hill, I realized they'd forgotten to crank up one of the windows. I yelled, "Window! Window! Window!" and they cranked it up just as we came into range of the camera. Sam looked at me with a smile and said, "Nice catch!"

Garrett seemed like he was still acting out Neal's character even inside the car. As the extra was hurrying across the street in front of us, he'd laugh and taunt, "You better hurry up there, girl! Get your butt off the street before I hit you!" On the last take, he almost did hit her, and she had to jump out of the way. Walter yelled, "That's a wrap!"

Sam and Garrett were like two kids together. They kept saying, "Can you believe we're in *On the Road?*" They were laughing like two boys who were playing hooky from school, or like two kids who'd just won the grand prize on some game show. They told me, "We have to keep telling ourselves we're actually here, acting in this movie. We can't believe how lucky we are."

Before I left, I showed Sam and Garrett the photograph of my mom I had brought along, tucked inside my bra, right next to my heart. I wanted to make sure that my mom got to take part in the movie. I was in the picture too; it was taken when my mom was about 60 and I was about 40. Sam commented, "Oh, she was lovely!" Then he seemed a little embarrassed, and said, "Of course, so are you!"

There was a funny moment later at the cast party at Francis Ford Coppola's restaurant, Café Zoetrope, in North Beach. The restaurant was closed to the public, and my friend Erin and I got there late, after the dinner had already been served. Carolyn Cassady was sitting in the back room, talking with Walter, Garrett, and some of the other celebrities. Roman Coppola was there too. I had never met Carolyn, so I went into the back room to introduce myself to her. She just kind of looked at me for a few minutes, as if she were trying to see my mother in me. "Oh, sit down, honey, oh please, we need to talk," she said finally. At that moment a couple of people came up to her and said, "You wanted a chance to smoke. The smokers are all going outside now." Then Garrett stood up and several of the others who were smokers too started for the door, and Carolyn got up and filed out with them. I never saw her again.

My mom told me that Carolyn had once said to her, as if she were apologizing for writing her book, "I had to sell this story—I have children to take care of." Carolyn chose to become famous, and she did. But she didn't have the ideal life. Being married to Neal wasn't easy. I think my mother probably had a better life than Carolyn did. But my mother was after something very different.

If my mother had wanted a life with Neal, it wouldn't have been the life of driving frantically around San Francisco looking for kicks, and it wouldn't have been the life Neal had later with Kesey and all those hippies taking acid on the bus. If Lu Anne could have had her dearest wish, Neal would have gone to college, he would have become the writer that he wanted to be. He wouldn't have become the Merry Prankster. If they had stayed together, this would not be the story.

That was Lu Anne's great sadness, that Neal didn't become everything she thought he could be, and that she didn't become everything she thought she could be with him. There was a song Barbra Streisand sang, an adaptation of Johnny Ashcroft's "Little Boy Lost," that hit my mom very hard when she heard it. That song was very profound for her, because the words were exactly what she felt for Neal. It went something like "Little boy lost / in search of little boy found / You go on wondering, wandering... / Why are you blind / to all you never were / really are / nearly are...." The song was about a boy, or it could be a man, who keeps searching for something that is really close by, but he never realizes it, and keeps wandering farther and farther from those things which are really most important to him.

My mom felt that Neal remained the Little Boy Lost, that he was never done traveling and "always unraveling," as the song says. For Lu Anne, that song was talking about how, after Jack's book came out, Neal was stuck in the role of the guy searching on the road, and he couldn't get beyond it. My mother told me that she and Neal were looking forward to everything in the early days. Everything was a possibility then—going to New York, becoming a writer. Neal was reaching for something better, and then somehow he got sidetracked. She said if she ever wrote the book about Neal, she would call it "Little Boy Lost."

The loss of Neal for Lu Anne wasn't like a daily loss, like the loss of someone who's been with you every day. They didn't interact that much during the later years of their lives. But it was the loss of youth, and the dream of youth, and the possibility of youth. When she lost Neal, all her youthful dreams were shut down. The future had been something that seemed open to her, and suddenly it was finalized—it was over. My mother wasn't visibly affected by his death—I mean, you didn't necessarily know by looking at her how much she was affected by it. But I'm sure that emotionally it affected her very much. Over the years, she talked about how he died too young, but the thing that bothered her the most was that he died *sad*. Their youth, their dream, was gone.

It's why when she was alone, when she was sick, she still needed contact with Neal. A lot of the time, he was hurting and lonely too. They reached out for each other at those times. When they were hurting and lonely, they would seek each other out. Even though they both had separate lives, in those moments when life was the hardest, they always reached out for that one other person they felt really knew them, understood them, and could comfort them. For Neal, it was always Lu Anne. And for Lu Anne, it was always Neal Cassady.

Neal Cassady, San Francisco, 1963. (Photo by Larry Keenan, Jr.)

About the Authors

⟹•⟸

 **GERALD NICOSIA** is a biographer, historian, poet, playwright, and novelist whose work has been closely associated with the Beat Movement as well as the 1960s. He came to prominence with the publication of *Memory Babe: A Critical Biography of Jack Kerouac* in 1983, a book that earned him the Distinguished Young Writer Award from the National Society of Arts and Letters while it was still a work in progress. It was highly praised by writers as diverse as John Rechy, Irving Stone, Bruce Cook, and Allen Ginsberg, who called it a "great book." Nicosia spent several decades in the Chicago and San Francisco literary scenes, making a name for himself as both a post-Beat poet and an organizer of marathon literary events, often in conjunction with the San Francisco Public Library and the Friends of the Library. He has been involved in several video and film projects, including the public television documentary *West Coast: Beat and Beyond*, directed by Chris

Felver, and the movie version of *On the Road,* directed by Walter Salles.

A lifelong friend of peace activist Ron Kovic, Nicosia spent decades studying, working with, and writing about Vietnam veterans in their long process of healing from that war. His definitive work on that subject, *Home to War: A History of the Vietnam Veterans' Movement,* was picked by the *Los Angeles Times* as one of the "Best Books of 2001," and has been praised by notable Vietnam veterans like John Kerry and Oliver Stone and also by veterans of America's later wars, such as Anthony Swofford, author of *Jarhead,* and leaders of Iraq and Afghanistan Veterans Against the War. He has taught Beat literature, the Sixties, and the Vietnam War literally around the world, including in China. His experiences in China, where he adopted his daughter Amy (Wu Ji), have found their way into a forthcoming book of poetry, *The China Poems.* He is also working on a book about racism and the death penalty in America, *Blackness Through the Land,* as well as a biography of Ntozake Shange titled *Beautiful, Colored, and Alive,* which will be published by St. Martin's Press.

ANNE MARIE SANTOS is the daughter of Lu Anne Henderson. She splits her time between Smithfield, Virginia, and San Francisco.

TO OUR READERS

Viva Editions publishes books that inform, enlighten, and entertain. We do our best to bring you, the reader, quality books that celebrate life, inspire the mind, revive the spirit, and enhance lives all around. Our authors are practical visionaries: people who offer deep wisdom in a hopeful and helpful manner. Viva was launched with an attitude of growth and we want to spread our joy and offer our support and advice where we can to help you live the Viva way: vivaciously!

We're grateful for all our readers and want to keep bringing you books for inspired living. We invite you to write to us with your comments and suggestions, and what you'd like to see more of. You can also sign up for our online newsletter to learn about new titles, author events, and special offers.

Viva Editions
2246 Sixth St.
Berkeley, CA 94710
www.vivaeditions.com
(800) 780-2279
Follow us on Twitter @vivaeditions
Friend/fan us on Facebook